MW01027428

CHURCH FATHERS AND TEACHERS

From Saint Leo the Great to Peter Lombard

POPE BENEDICT XVI

CHURCH FATHERS AND TEACHERS

From Saint Leo the Great to Peter Lombard

General Audiences
5 March 2008–25 June 2008
11 February 2009–17 June 2009
2 September 2009–30 December 2009

IGNATIUS PRESS   SAN FRANCISCO

English translation by *L'Osservatore Romano*

Cover art:
From The Life of Saint Benedict
(From a series of paintings completed between 1497–1508)
Saint Benedict Instructing the People in Sacred Doctrine
By Sodoma (Bazzi), Giovanni Antonio
Abbey, Monte Oliveto Maggiore, Italy
© Erich Lessing/Art Resource, New York

Papal coat of arms image by www.AgnusImages.com

Cover design by Roxanne Mei Lum

© 2010 by Libreria Editrice Vaticana, Vatican City
All rights reserved
ISBN 978-1-58617-317-3
Library of Congress Control Number 2010922762
Printed in the United States of America ∞

CONTENTS

1. Saint Leo the Great   7

2. Boethius and Cassiodorus   12

3. Saint Benedict of Norcia   19

4. Pseudo-Dionysius the Areopagite   25

5. Saint Romanus the Melodist   31

6. Saint Gregory the Great (1)   37

7. Saint Gregory the Great (2)   43

8. Saint Columban   49

9. Saint Isidore of Seville   55

10. Saint Maximus the Confessor   60

11. John Climacus   66

12. Saint Bede, the Venerable   73

13. Saint Boniface, the Apostle of the Germans   79

14. Ambrose Autpert   86

15. Germanus of Constantinople   93

16. John Damascene   99

17. Saint Theodore the Studite   105

18. Rabanus Maurus   111

19. John Scotus Erigena   117

20. Saints Cyril and Methodius   123

21. Saint Odo of Cluny   129

22. Saint Peter Damian   135

23. Symeon the New Theologian   141

24. Saint Anselm   146

25. Peter the Venerable   152

26. Saint Bernard of Clairvaux   157

27. Monastic Theology and Scholastic Theology   163

28. Two Theological Models in Comparison:
    Bernard and Abelard   169

29. The Cluniac Reform   174

30. The Cathedral from the Romanesque to the
    Gothic Architecture: The Theological
    Background   179

31. Hugh and Richard of Saint-Victor   185

32. William of Saint-Thierry   192

33. Rupert of Deutz   198

34. John of Salisbury   204

35. Peter Lombard   210

Saint Leo the Great

WEDNESDAY, 5 MARCH 2008
Paul VI Audience Hall

Dear Brothers and Sisters,

Continuing our journey through the Fathers of the Church, true stars that shine in the distance, at our meeting today we encounter a Pope who in 1754 Benedict XIV proclaimed a Doctor of the Church: Saint Leo the Great. As the title soon attributed to him by tradition suggests, he was truly one of the greatest Pontiffs to have honored the Roman See and made a very important contribution to strengthening its authority and prestige. He was the first Bishop of Rome to have been called Leo, a name used subsequently by another twelve Supreme Pontiffs, and was also the first Pope whose preaching to the people who gathered around him during celebrations has come down to us. We spontaneously think of him also in the context of today's Wednesday General Audiences, events that in past decades have become a customary meeting of the Bishop of Rome with the faithful and the many visitors from every part of the world.

Leo was a Tuscan native. In about the year 430 A.D., he became a deacon of the Church of Rome, in which he acquired over time a very important position. In the year

440 his prominent role induced Galla Placidia, who then ruled the Empire of the West, to send him to Gaul to heal a difficult situation. But in the summer of that year, Pope Sixtus III, whose name is associated with the magnificent mosaics in Saint Mary Major's, died, and it was Leo who was elected to succeed him. Leo heard the news precisely while he was carrying out his peace mission in Gaul. Having returned to Rome, the new Pope was consecrated on 29 September 440. This is how his Pontificate began. It lasted more than twenty-one years and was undoubtedly one of the most important in the Church's history. Pope Leo died on 10 November 461 and was buried near the tomb of Saint Peter. Today, his relics are preserved in one of the altars in the Vatican Basilica.

The times in which Pope Leo lived were very difficult: constant barbarian invasions, the gradual weakening of imperial authority in the West, and the long, drawn-out social crisis forced the Bishop of Rome—as was to happen even more obviously a century and a half later during the Pontificate of Gregory the Great—to play an important role in civil and political events. This, naturally, could only add to the importance and prestige of the Roman See. The fame of one particular episode in Leo's life has endured. It dates back to 452, when the Pope, together with a Roman delegation, met Attila, chief of the Huns, in Mantua and dissuaded him from continuing the war of invasion by which he had already devastated the northeastern regions of Italy. Thus, he saved the rest of the Peninsula. This important event soon became memorable and lives on as an emblematic sign of the Pontiff's action for peace. Unfortunately, the outcome of another Papal initiative three years later was not as successful, yet it was a sign of courage that still amazes us: in the spring of 455 Leo did not manage to prevent

Genseric's Vandals, who had reached the gates of Rome, from invading the undefended city that they plundered for two weeks. This gesture of the Pope—who, defenseless and surrounded by his clergy, went forth to meet the invader to implore him to desist—nevertheless prevented Rome from being burned and assured that the Basilicas of Saint Peter, Saint Paul, and Saint John, in which part of the terrified population sought refuge, were spared.

We are familiar with Pope Leo's action thanks to his most beautiful sermons—almost one hundred in a splendid and clear Latin have been preserved—and thanks to his approximately 150 letters. In these texts the Pontiff appears in all his greatness, devoted to the service of truth in charity through an assiduous exercise of the Word which shows him to us as both theologian and pastor. Leo the Great, constantly thoughtful of his faithful and of the people of Rome but also of communion between the different Churches and of their needs, was a tireless champion and upholder of the Roman Primacy, presenting himself as the Apostle Peter's authentic heir: the many Bishops who gathered at the Council of Chalcedon, the majority of whom came from the East, were well aware of this.

This Council, held in 451 and in which 350 Bishops took part, was the most important assembly ever to have been celebrated in the history of the Church. Chalcedon represents the actual Christological goal of the three previous Ecumenical Councils: Nicaea in 325, Constantinople in 381, and Ephesus in 431. By the sixth century these four Councils that sum up the faith of the ancient Church were already being compared to the four Gospels. This is what Gregory the Great affirms in a famous letter (I, 24): "I confess that I receive and revere, as the four books of the Gospel, so also the four Councils", because on them,

Gregory explains further, "as on a four-square stone, rises the structure of the holy faith". The Council of Chalcedon, which rejected the heresy of Eutyches, who denied the true human nature of the Son of God, affirmed the union in his one Person, without confusion and without separation, of his two natures, human and divine.

The Pope asserted this faith in Jesus Christ, true God and true man, in an important doctrinal text addressed to the Bishop of Constantinople, the so-called *Tome to Flavian*, which, read at Chalcedon, was received by the Bishops present with an eloquent acclamation. Information on it has been preserved in the proceedings of the Council: "Peter has spoken through the mouth of Leo", the Council Fathers announced in unison. From this intervention in particular, but also from others made during the Christological controversy in those years, it is clear that the Pope felt with special urgency his responsibilities as Successor of Peter, whose role in the Church is unique, since "to one Apostle alone was entrusted what was communicated to all the Apostles", as Leo said in one of his sermons for the Feast of Saints Peter and Paul (83, 2). And the Pontiff was able to exercise these responsibilities, in the West as in the East, intervening in various circumstances with caution, firmness, and lucidity through his writings and legates. In this manner he showed how exercising the Roman Primacy was as necessary then as it is today to serve communion, a characteristic of Christ's one Church, effectively.

Aware of the historical period in which he lived and of the change that was taking place—from pagan Rome to Christian Rome—in a period of profound crisis, Leo the Great knew how to make himself close to the people and the faithful with his pastoral action and his preaching. He enlivened charity in a Rome tried by famines, an influx of

refugees, injustice, and poverty. He opposed pagan super-
stitions and the actions of Manichaean groups. He associated the liturgy with the daily life of Christians: for example,
by combining the practice of fasting with charity and almsgiving above all on the occasion of the *Quattro tempora*, which
in the course of the year marked the change of seasons. In
particular, Leo the Great taught his faithful—and his words
still apply for us today—that the Christian liturgy is not the
memory of past events, but the actualization of invisible
realities which act in the lives of each one of us. This is
what he stressed in a sermon (cf. 64, 1–2) on Easter, to be
celebrated in every season of the year, "not so much as
something of the past as rather an event of the present". All
this fits into a precise project, the Holy Pontiff insisted: just
as, in fact, the Creator enlivened with the breath of rational
life man formed from the dust of the ground, after the original sin he sent his Son into the world to restore to man his
lost dignity and to destroy the dominion of the devil through
the new life of grace.

This is the Christological mystery to which Saint Leo
the Great, with his Letter to the Council of Ephesus, made
an effective and essential contribution, confirming for all
time—through this Council—what Saint Peter said at Cae-
sarea Philippi. With Peter and as Peter, he professed: "You
are the Christ, the Son of the living God." And so it is that
God and man together "are not foreign to the human race
but alien to sin" (cf. *Serm.* 64). Through the force of this
Christological faith, he was a great messenger of peace and
love. He thus shows us the way: in faith we learn charity.
Let us therefore learn with Saint Leo the Great to believe
in Christ, true God and true man, and to implement this
faith every day in action for peace and love of neighbor.

2

Boethius and Cassiodorus

WEDNESDAY, 12 MARCH 2008
Paul VI Audience Hall

Dear Brothers and Sisters,

Today, I would like to talk about two ecclesiastical writers, Boethius and Cassiodorus, who lived in some of the most turbulent years in the Christian West and in the Italian Peninsula in particular. Odoacer, King of the Rugians, a Germanic race, had rebelled, putting an end to the Western Roman Empire (476 A.D.), but it was not long before he was killed by Theodoric's Ostrogoths, who had controlled the Italian Peninsula for some decades. Boethius, born in Rome in about 480 from the noble Anicius lineage, entered public life when he was still young and by age twenty-five was already a senator. Faithful to his family's tradition, he devoted himself to politics, convinced that it would be possible to temper the fundamental structure of Roman society with the values of the new peoples. And in this new time of cultural encounter he considered it his role to reconcile and bring together these two cultures, the classical Roman and the nascent Ostrogoth culture. Thus, he was also politically active under Theodoric, who at the outset held him in high esteem. In spite of this public activity, Boethius did not neglect his studies and dedicated himself in particular to acquiring a deep knowledge of philosophical and religious subjects. However, he also wrote manuals on arithmetic, geometry, music, and astronomy, all with the intention of passing on the great Greco-Roman culture to the new generations, to the new times. In this context, in his commitment to fostering the encounter of cultures, he used the categories of Greek philosophy to present the Christian faith, here too seeking a synthesis between the Hellenistic-Roman heritage and the Gospel message. For this very reason Boethius was described as the last representative of ancient Roman culture and the first of the medieval intellectuals.

His most famous work is undoubtedly *De Consolatione Philosophiae*, which he wrote in prison to help explain his unjust detention. In fact, he had been accused of plotting against King Theodoric for having taken the side of his friend Senator Albinus in a court case. But this was a pretext. Actually, Theodoric, an Arian and a barbarian, suspected that Boethius was sympathizing with the Byzantine Emperor Justinian. Boethius was tried and sentenced to death. He was executed on 23 October 524, when he was only forty-four years old. It is precisely because of his tragic end that he can also speak from the heart of his own experience to contemporary man, and especially to the multitudes who suffer the same fate because of the injustice inherent in so much of "human justice". Through this work, *De Consolatione Philosophiae*, he sought consolation, enlightenment, and wisdom in prison. And he said that precisely in this situation he knew how to distinguish between apparent goods, which disappear in prison, and true goods, such as genuine friendship, which even in prison do not disappear. The loftiest good is God: Boethius—and he teaches us this—learned not to sink into a fatalism that extinguishes hope. He teaches us that it is not the event but Providence that governs, and Providence has a face. It is possible to speak to Providence because Providence is God. Thus, even in prison, he was left with the possibility of prayer, of dialogue with the One who saves us. At the same time, even in this situation he retained his sense of the beauty of culture and remembered the teaching of the great ancient Greek and Roman philosophers, such as Plato, Aristotle—he had begun to translate these Greeks into Latin—Cicero, Seneca, and also poets, such as Tibullus and Virgil.

Boethius held that philosophy, in the sense of the quest for true wisdom, was the true medicine of the soul (Bk I). On the other hand, man can experience authentic happiness only within his own interiority (Bk II). Boethius thus succeeded in finding meaning by thinking of his own personal tragedy in the light of a sapiential text of the Old Testament (Wis 7:30—8:1) which he cites: "Against wisdom evil does not prevail. She reaches mightily from one end of the earth to the other, and she orders all things well" (Bk III, 12: *PL* 63, 780). The so-called prosperity of the wicked is therefore proven to be false (Bk IV), and the providential nature of *adversa fortuna* is highlighted. Life's difficulties not only reveal how transient and short-lived life is, but are even shown to serve for identifying and preserving authentic relations among human beings. *Adversa fortuna*, in fact, makes it possible to discern false friends from true and makes one realize that nothing is more precious to the human being than a true friendship. The fatalistic acceptance of a condition of suffering is nothing short of perilous, the believer Boethius added, because "it eliminates at its roots the very possibility of prayer and of theological hope, which form the basis of man's relationship with God" (Bk V, 3: *PL* 63, 842).

The final peroration of *De Consolatione Philosophiae* can be considered a synthesis of the entire teaching that Boethius addressed to himself and all who might find themselves in his same conditions. Thus, in prison he wrote: "So combat vices, dedicate yourselves to a virtuous life oriented by hope, which draws the heart upward until it reaches Heaven with prayers nourished by humility. Should you refuse to lie, the imposition you have suffered can change into the enormous advantage of always having before your eyes the supreme Judge, who sees and knows how things truly are" (Bk V, 6: *PL* 63, 862). Every prisoner, regardless of the reason why he ended up in prison, senses how burdensome this particular human condition is, especially when it is brutalized, as it was for Boethius, by recourse to torture. Then particularly absurd is the condition of those like Boethius—whom the city of Pavia recognizes and celebrates in the liturgy as a martyr of the faith—who are tortured to death for no other reason than their own ideals and political and religious convictions. Boethius, the symbol of an immense number of people unjustly imprisoned in all ages and on all latitudes, is in fact an objective entrance way that gives access to contemplation of the mysterious Crucified One of Golgotha.

Marcus Aurelius Cassiodorus was a contemporary of Boethius, a Calabrian born in Scyllacium in about 485 A.D. and who died at a very advanced age in Vivarium in 580. Cassiodorus, a man with a privileged social status, likewise devoted himself to political life and cultural commitment as few others in the Roman West of his time. Perhaps the only men who could stand on an equal footing in this two-fold interest were Boethius, whom we have mentioned, and Gregory the Great, the future Pope of Rome (590–604). Aware of the need to prevent all the human and humanist patrimony accumulated in the golden age of the Roman Empire from vanishing into oblivion, Cassiodorus collaborated generously, and with the highest degree of political responsibility, with the new peoples who had crossed the boundaries of the Empire and settled in Italy. He, too, was a model of cultural encounter, of dialogue, of reconciliation. Historical events did not permit him to make his political and cultural dreams come true; he wanted to create a synthesis between the Roman and Christian traditions of Italy and the new culture of the Goths. These same events, however, convinced him of the providentiality of the monastic movement that was putting down roots in Christian lands. He decided to support it and gave it all his material wealth and spiritual energy.

He conceived the idea of entrusting to the monks the task of recovering, preserving, and transmitting to those to come the immense cultural patrimony of the ancients so that it would not be lost. For this reason he founded *Vivarium*, a coenobitic community in which everything was organized in such a way that the monk's intellectual work was esteemed as precious and indispensable. He arranged that even those monks who had no academic training must be involved, not solely in physical labor and farming, but also in transcribing manuscripts and thus helping to transmit the great culture to future generations. And this was by no means at the expense of monastic and Christian spiritual dedication or of charitable activity for the poor. In his teaching, expounded in various works but especially in the Treatise *De Anima* and in the *Institutiones Divinarum Litterarum* (cf. *PL* 69, 1108), prayer nourished by Sacred Scripture and particularly by assiduous recourse to the Psalms (cf. *PL* 69, 1149) always has a central place as the essential sustenance for all. Thus, for example, this most learned Calabrian introduced his *Expositio in Psalterium*: "Having rejected and abandoned in Ravenna the demands of a political career marked by the disgusting taste of worldly concerns, having enjoyed the Psalter, a book that came from Heaven, as true honey of the soul, I dived into it avidly, thirsting to examine it without a pause, to steep myself in that salutary sweetness, having had enough of the countless disappointments of active life" (*PL* 70, 10).

The search for God, the aspiration to contemplate him, Cassiodorus notes, continues to be the permanent goal of monastic life (cf. *PL* 69, 1107). Nonetheless, he adds that with the help of divine grace (cf. *PL* 69, 1131, 1142), greater profit can be attained from the revealed Word with the use of scientific discoveries and the "profane" cultural means that were possessed in the past by the Greeks and Romans (cf. *PL* 69, 1140). Personally, Cassiodorus dedicated himself to philosophical, theological, and exegetical studies without any special creativity, but he was attentive to the insights he considered valid in others. He read Jerome and Augustine in particular with respect and devotion. Of the latter he said: "In Augustine there is such a great wealth of writings that it seems to me impossible to find anything that has not already been abundantly treated by him" (cf. *PL* 70, 10). Citing Jerome, on the other hand, he urged the monks of *Vivarium*:

> It is not only those who fight to the point of bloodshed or who live in virginity who win the palm of victory but also all who, with God's help, triumph over physical vices and preserve their upright faith. But in order that you may always, with God's help, more easily overcome the world's pressures and enticements while remaining in it as pilgrims constantly journeying forward, seek first to guarantee for yourselves the salutary help suggested by the first Psalm, which recommends meditation night and day on the law of the Lord. Indeed, the enemy will not find any gap through which to assault you if all your attention is

taken up by Christ. (*De Institutione Divinarum Scripturarum*, 32: *PL* 69, 1147)

This is a recommendation we can also accept as valid. In fact, we live in a time of intercultural encounter, of the danger of violence that destroys cultures, and of the necessary commitment to pass on important values and to teach the new generations the path of reconciliation and peace. We find this path by turning to the God with the human Face, the God who revealed himself to us in Christ.

3

Saint Benedict of Norcia

WEDNESDAY, 9 APRIL 2008
Saint Peter's Square

Dear Brothers and Sisters,

Today, I would like to speak about Benedict, the Founder of Western Monasticism and also the Patron of my Pontificate. I begin with words that Saint Gregory the Great wrote about Saint Benedict: "The man of God who shone on this earth among so many miracles was just as brilliant in the eloquent exposition of his teaching" (cf. *II Dialogues* 36). The great Pope wrote these words in 592 A.D. The holy monk, who had died barely fifty years earlier, lived on in people's memories and especially in the flourishing religious Order he had founded. Saint Benedict of Norcia, with his life and his work, had a fundamental influence on the development of European civilization and culture. The most important source on Benedict's life is the second book of Saint Gregory the Great's *Dialogues*. It is not a biography in the classical sense. In accordance with the ideas of his time, by giving the example of a real man—Saint Benedict, in this case—Gregory wished to illustrate the ascent to the peak of contemplation which can be achieved by those who abandon themselves to God. He therefore gives us a model for human life in the climb toward the summit of perfection. Saint Gregory the Great also tells in this book of the *Dialogues* of many miracles worked by the Saint, and here too he does not wish merely to recount something curious but rather to show how God, by admonishing, helping, and even punishing, intervenes in the practical situations of man's life. Gregory's aim was to demonstrate that God is not a distant hypothesis placed at the origin of the world but is present in the life of man, of every man.

This perspective of the "biographer" is also explained in light of the general context of his time: straddling the fifth and sixth centuries, "the world was overturned by a tremendous crisis of values and institutions caused by the collapse of the Roman Empire, the invasion of new peoples, and the decay of morals." But in this terrible situation, here, in this very city of Rome, Gregory presented Saint Benedict as a "luminous star" in order to point the way out of the "black night of history" (cf. John Paul II, 18 May 1979). In fact, the Saint's work and particularly his *Rule* were to prove heralds of an authentic spiritual leaven which, in the course of the centuries, far beyond the boundaries of his country and time, changed the face of Europe following the fall of the political unity created by the Roman Empire, inspiring a new spiritual and cultural unity, that of the Christian faith shared by the peoples of the Continent. This is how the reality we call "Europe" came into being.

Saint Benedict was born around the year 480. As Saint Gregory said, he came "*ex provincia Nursiae*"—from the province of Norcia. His well-to-do parents sent him to study in Rome. However, he did not stay long in the Eternal City. As a fully plausible explanation, Gregory mentions that the young Benedict was put off by the dissolute life-style of many of his fellow students and did not wish to make the same mistakes. He wanted only to please God: "*soli Deo placere desiderans*" (*II Dialogues*, Prol. 1). Thus, even before he finished his studies, Benedict left Rome and withdrew to the solitude of the mountains east of Rome. After a short stay in the village of Enfide (today, Affile), where for a time he lived with a "religious community" of monks, he became a hermit in the neighboring locality of Subiaco. He lived there completely alone for three years in a cave which has been the heart of a Benedictine Monastery called the "Sacro Speco" (Holy Grotto) since the early Middle Ages. The period in Subiaco, a time of solitude with God, was a time of maturation for Benedict. It was here that he bore and overcame the three fundamental temptations of every human being: the temptation of self-affirmation and the desire to put oneself at the center, the temptation of sensuality, and, lastly, the temptation of anger and revenge. In fact, Benedict was convinced that only after overcoming these temptations would he be able to say a useful word to others about their own situations of neediness. Thus, having tranquilized his soul, he could be in full control of the drive of his ego and thus create peace around him. Only then did he decide to found his first monasteries in the Valley of the Anio, near Subiaco.

In the year 529, Benedict left Subiaco and settled in Monte Cassino. Some have explained this move as an escape from the intrigues of an envious local cleric. However, this attempt at an explanation hardly proved convincing since the latter's sudden death did not induce Benedict to return (*II Dialogues* 8). In fact, this decision was called for because he had entered a new phase of inner maturity and monastic experience. According to Gregory the Great, Benedict's exodus from the remote Valley of the Anio to Monte Cassino—a plateau dominating the vast surrounding plain which can be seen from afar—has a symbolic character: a hidden monastic life has its own *raison d'être*, but a monastery also has its public purpose in the life of the Church and of society, and it must give visibility to the faith as a force of life. Indeed, when Benedict's earthly life ended on 21 March 547, he bequeathed with his *Rule* and the Benedictine family he founded a heritage that bore fruit in the passing centuries and is still bearing fruit throughout the world.

Throughout the second book of his *Dialogues*, Gregory shows us how Saint Benedict's life was steeped in an atmosphere of prayer, the foundation of his existence. Without prayer there is no experience of God. Yet Benedict's spirituality was not an interiority removed from reality. In the anxiety and confusion of his day, he lived under God's gaze and in this very way never lost sight of the duties of daily life and of man with his practical needs. Seeing God, he understood the reality of man and his mission. In his *Rule* he describes monastic life as "a school for the service of the Lord" (Prol. 45) and advises his monks, "let nothing be preferred to the Work of God" [that is, the Divine Office, or the Liturgy of the Hours] (43, 3). However, Benedict states that in the first place prayer is an act of listening (Prol. 9–11), which must then be expressed in action. "The Lord is waiting every day for us to respond to his holy admonitions by our deeds" (Prol. 35). Thus, the monk's life becomes a fruitful symbiosis between action and contemplation, "so that God may be glorified in all things" (57, 9). In contrast with a facile and egocentric self-fulfillment, today often exalted, the first and indispensable commitment of a disciple of Saint Benedict is the sincere search for God (58, 7) on the path mapped out by the humble and obedient Christ (5, 13), whose love he must put before all else (4, 21; 72, 11), and in this way, in the service of the other, he becomes a man of service and peace. In the exercise of obedience practiced by faith inspired by love (5, 2), the monk achieves humility (5, 1), to which the *Rule* dedicates an entire chapter (7). In this way, man conforms ever more to Christ and attains true self-fulfillment as a creature in the image and likeness of God.

The obedience of the disciple must correspond with the wisdom of the Abbot, who, in the monastery, "is believed to hold the place of Christ" (2, 2; 63, 13). The figure of the Abbot, which is described above all in Chapter 2 of the *Rule* with a profile of spiritual beauty and demanding commitment, can be considered a self-portrait of Benedict, since, as Saint Gregory the Great wrote, "the holy man could not teach otherwise than as he himself lived" (cf. *II Dialogues* 36). The Abbot must be at the same time a tender father and a strict teacher (cf. 2, 24), a true educator. Inflexible against vices, he is nevertheless called above all to imitate the tenderness of the Good Shepherd (27, 8), to "serve rather than to rule" (64, 8) in order "to show them all what is good and holy by his deeds more than by his words" and "illustrate the divine precepts by his example" (2, 12). To be able to decide responsibly, the Abbot must also be a person who listens to "the brethren's views" (3, 2), because "the Lord often reveals to the youngest what is best" (3, 3). This provision makes a *Rule* written almost fifteen centuries ago surprisingly modern! A man with public responsibility even in small circles must always be a man who can listen and learn from what he hears.

Benedict describes the *Rule* he wrote as "minimal, just an initial outline" (cf. 73, 8); in fact, however, he offers useful guidelines not only for monks but for all who seek guidance on their journey toward God. For its moderation, humanity, and sober discernment between the essential and the secondary in the spiritual life, his *Rule* has retained its illuminating power even to today. By proclaiming Saint Benedict

Patron of Europe on 24 October 1964, Paul VI intended to recognize the marvelous work the Saint achieved with his *Rule* for the formation of the civilization and culture of Europe. Having recently emerged from a century that was deeply wounded by two World Wars and the collapse of the great ideologies, now revealed as tragic utopias, Europe today is in search of its own identity. Of course, in order to create new and lasting unity, political, economic, and juridical instruments are important, but it is also necessary to awaken an ethical and spiritual renewal which draws on the Christian roots of the Continent; otherwise a new Europe cannot be built. Without this vital sap, man is exposed to the danger of succumbing to the ancient temptation of seeking to redeem himself by himself—a utopia which in different ways, in twentieth-century Europe, as Pope John Paul II pointed out, has caused "a regression without precedent in the tormented history of humanity" (*Address to the Pontifical Council for Culture*, 12 January 1990). Today, in seeking true progress, let us also listen to the *Rule* of Saint Benedict as a guiding light on our journey. The great monk is still a true master at whose school we can learn to become proficient in true humanism.

4

Pseudo-Dionysius the Areopagite

WEDNESDAY, 14 MAY 2008
Saint Peter's Square

Dear Brothers and Sisters,

In the course of the Catechesis on the Fathers of the Church, today I would like to speak of a rather mysterious figure: a sixth-century theologian whose name is unknown and who wrote under the pseudonym of Dionysius the Areopagite. With this pseudonym he was alluding to the passage of Scripture we have just heard, the event recounted by Saint Luke in chapter 17 of the Acts of the Apostles, where he tells how Paul preached in Athens at the Areopagus to an elite group of the important Greek intellectual world. In the end, the majority of his listeners proved not to be interested and went away jeering at him. Yet some, Saint Luke says a few, approached Paul and opened themselves to the faith. The Evangelist gives us two names: Dionysius, a member of the Areopagus, and a woman named Damaris.

If five centuries later the author of these books chose the pseudonym "Dionysius the Areopagite", it means that his intention was to put Greek wisdom at the service of the Gospel, to foster the encounter of Greek culture and intelligence with the proclamation of Christ; he wanted to do what this Dionysius had intended, that is, to make Greek thought converge with Saint Paul's proclamation; being a Greek, he wanted to become a disciple of Saint Paul, hence a disciple of Christ.

Why did he hide his name and choose this pseudonym? One part of the answer I have already given: he wanted, precisely, to express this fundamental intention of his thought. But there are two hypotheses concerning this anonymity and pseudonym. The first hypothesis says that it was a deliberate falsification by which, in dating his works back to the first century, to the time of Saint Paul, he wished to give his literary opus a quasi-apostolic authority. But there is another better hypothesis than this, which seems to me barely credible: namely, that he himself desired to make an act of humility; he did not want to glorify his own name; he wanted, not to build a monument to himself with his work, but rather truly to serve the Gospel, to create an ecclesial theology, neither individual nor based on himself. Actually, he succeeded in elaborating a theology which, of course, we can date to the sixth century but cannot attribute to any of the figures of that period: it is a somewhat "de-individualized" theology, that is, a theology which expresses a common thought and language. It was a period of fierce polemics following the Council of Chalcedon; indeed, he said in his *Seventh Epistle*: "I do not wish to spark polemics; I simply speak of the truth, I seek the truth." And the light of truth by itself causes errors to fall away and makes what is good shine forth. And with this principle he purified Greek thought and related it to the Gospel. This principle, which he affirms in his seventh letter, is also the expression of a true spirit of dialogue: it is about, not seeking the things that separate, but seeking the truth in Truth itself. This then radiates and causes errors to fade away.

Therefore, although this author's theology is, so to speak, "supra-personal", truly ecclesial, we can place it in the sixth century. Why? The Greek spirit, which he placed at the service of the Gospel, he encountered in the books of Proclus, who died in Athens in 485. This author belonged to late Platonism, a current of thought which had transformed Plato's philosophy into a sort of religion, whose ultimate purpose was to create a great apologetic for Greek polytheism and return, following Christianity's success, to the ancient Greek religion. He wanted to demonstrate that, in reality, the divinities were the active forces in the cosmos. The consequence to be drawn from this was that polytheism must be considered truer than monotheism with its single Creator God. What Proclus was demonstrating was a great cosmic system of divinity, of mysterious forces, through which, in this deified cosmos, man could find access to the divinity. However, he made a distinction between paths for the simple, who were incapable of rising to the heights of truth—certain rites could suffice for them—and paths for the wise, who were to purify themselves to arrive at the pure light.

As can be seen, this thought is profoundly anti-Christian. It is a late reaction to the triumph of Christianity, an anti-Christian use of Plato, whereas a Christian interpretation of the great philosopher was already in course. It is interesting that this Pseudo-Dionysius dared to avail himself of this very thought to demonstrate the truth of Christ; to transform this polytheistic universe into a cosmos created by God, into the harmony of God's cosmos, where every force is praise of God, and to show this great harmony, this symphony of the cosmos that goes from the Seraphim to the Angels and Archangels, to man and to all the creatures which, together, reflect God's beauty and are praise of God.

He thus transformed the polytheistic image into a praise of the Creator and his creature. In this way we can discover the essential characteristics of his thought: first and foremost, it is cosmic praise. All Creation speaks of God and is praise of God. Since the creature is praise of God, Pseudo-Dionysius' theology became a liturgical theology: God is found above all in praising him, not only in reflection; and the liturgy is not something made by us, something invented in order to have a religious experience for a certain period of time; it is singing with the choir of creatures and entering into cosmic reality itself. And in this very way the liturgy, apparently only ecclesiastical, becomes expansive and great; it becomes our union with the language of all creatures. He says: God cannot be spoken of in an abstract way; speaking of God is always—he says, using a Greek word—a "*hymnein*", singing for God with the great hymn of the creatures which is reflected and made concrete in liturgical praise. Yet, although his theology is cosmic, ecclesial, and liturgical, it is also profoundly personal. He created the first great mystical theology. Indeed, with him the word "mystic" acquires a new meaning. Until then for Christians such a word was equivalent to the word "sacramental", that is, what pertains to the "*mysterion*", to the sacrament. With him the word "mystic" becomes more personal, more intimate: it expresses the soul's journey toward God. And how can God be found? Here we note once again an important element in his dialogue between Greek philosophy and Christianity and, in particular, biblical faith. Apparently what Plato says and what the great philosophy on God says is far loftier, far truer; the Bible appears somewhat "barbaric", simple or pre-critical, one might say today; but he remarks that precisely this is necessary, so that in this way we can understand that the loftiest concepts of God never reach his true grandeur: they always fall short of it. In fact these images enable us to understand that God is above every concept; in the simplicity of the images we find more truth than in great concepts. The Face of God is our inability to express truly what he is. In this way one speaks—and Pseudo-Dionysius himself speaks—of a "negative theology". It is easier for us to say what God is not rather than to say what he truly is. Only through these images can we intuit his true Face; moreover, this Face of God is very concrete: it is Jesus Christ.

And although Dionysius shows us, following Proclus, the harmony of the heavenly choirs in such a way that it seems that they all depend on one another, it is true that on our journey toward God we are still very far from him. Pseudo-Dionysius shows that in the end the journey to God is God himself, who makes himself close to us in Jesus Christ. Thus, a great and mysterious theology also becomes very concrete, both in the interpretation of the liturgy and in the discourse on Jesus Christ: with all this, Dionysius the Areopagite exerted a strong influence on all medieval theology and on all mystical theology, both in the East and in the West. He was virtually rediscovered in the thirteenth century, especially by Saint Bonaventure, the great Franciscan theologian, who in this mystical theology found the conceptual instrument for reinterpreting the heritage—so simple and profound—of Saint Francis. Together with Dionysius, the "Poverello" tells us that in the end love sees more than reason. Where the light of love shines, the shadows of reason are dispelled; love sees; love is an eye, and experience gives us more than reflection. Bonaventure saw in Saint Francis what this experience is: it is the experience of a very humble, very realistic journey, day by day; it is walking with Christ, accepting his Cross. In this poverty and in this humility, in the humility that is also lived in ecclesiality, is an experience of God which is loftier than that attained by reflection. In it we really touch God's Heart.

Today Dionysius the Areopagite has a new relevance: he appears as a great mediator in the modern dialogue between Christianity and the mystical theologies of Asia, whose characteristic feature is the conviction that it is impossible to say who God is, that only indirect things can be said about him; that God can be spoken of only with the "not", and that it is only possible to reach him by entering into this indirect experience of "not". And here a similarity can be seen between the thought of the Areopagite and that of Asian religions; he can be a mediator today as he was between the Greek spirit and the Gospel.

In this context it can be seen that dialogue does not accept superficiality. It is precisely when one enters into the depths of the encounter with Christ that an ample space for dialogue also opens. When one encounters the light of truth, one realizes that it is a light for everyone; polemics disappear, and it is possible to understand one another, or at least to speak to one another, to come closer. The path of dialogue consists precisely in being close to God in Christ, in a deep encounter with him, in the experience of the truth which opens us to the light and helps us reach out to others—with the light of truth, the light of love. And in the end, he tells us: take the path of experience, the humble experience of faith, every day. Then the heart is enlarged and can see and also illumine reason so that it perceives God's beauty. Let us pray to the Lord to help us today, too, to place the wisdom of our day at the service of the Gospel, discovering ever anew the beauty of faith, the encounter with God in Christ.

5

Saint Romanus the Melodist

WEDNESDAY, 21 MAY 2008
Paul VI Audience Hall

Dear Brothers and Sisters,

In the series of Catecheses on the Fathers of the Church, I would like today to talk about a little-known figure: Romanus the Melodist, who was born in about 490 in Emesa (today Homs), in Syria. Theologian, poet, and composer, he belonged to the great ranks of theologians who transformed theology into poetry. Let us think of his compatriot, Saint Ephrem the Syrian, who lived two hundred years before him. However, we can also think of Western theologians, such as Saint Ambrose, whose hymns are still part of our liturgy and still move hearts; or of a theologian, a very vigorous thinker such as Saint Thomas, who gave us hymns for the *Feast of Corpus Christi* [to be celebrated] tomorrow; we think of Saint John of the Cross and of so many others. Faith is love and therefore creates poetry and music. Faith is joy; therefore it creates beauty.

Thus Romanus the Melodist is one of these, a poet theologian and composer. Having acquired the rudiments of Greek and Syrian culture in his native town, he moved to Berytus (Beirut), perfecting there his classical education and his knowledge of rhetoric. After being ordained a permanent deacon (ca. 515), he was a preacher here for three years. He then moved to Constantinople toward the end of the reign of Anastasius I (ca. 518) and settled there in the monastery adjacent to the Church of the *Theotokos*, the Mother of God. It was here that the key episode of his life occurred: the *Synaxarion* [The Lives of the Orthodox Saints] informs us of the apparition of the Mother of God in a dream and of the gift of the poetic charism. In fact, Mary enjoined him to swallow a scroll. On awakening the following morning—it was the Feast of the Nativity of the Lord—Romanus began declaiming from the ambo: "Today the Virgin gives birth to the Transcendent" (Hymn "*On the Nativity*", I. *Proemio*). So it was that he became a homilist-cantor until his death (after 555).

Romanus lives on in history as one of the most representative authors of liturgical hymns. At that time the homily was virtually the only opportunity for catechetical instruction afforded to the faithful. Thus, Romanus is an eminent witness of the religious feeling of his epoch, but also of a lively and original catechesis. In his compositions we can appreciate the creativity of this form of catechesis, the creativity of the theological thought and aesthetics and sacred hymnography of that time. The place in which Romanus preached was a sanctuary on the outskirts of Constantinople: he would mount the ambo that stood in the center of the church and speak to the community utilizing a somewhat extravagant technique: he referred to the mural depictions or icons arranged on the ambo and even made use of dialogue. He sang his homilies in metric verse known as *kontakia*. The term *kontakion*, "little rod", would seem to refer to the staff around which a liturgical or other manuscript was wound. Eighty-nine *kontakia* bearing Romanus' name have come down to us, but tradition attributes one thousand to him.

In the works of Romanus, each *kontakion* is composed, in most cases, of between eighteen and twenty-four strophes, with an equal number of syllables, structured on the model of the first strophe, the *irmo*. The rhythmic accents in the verses of all the strophes are modeled on those of the *irmo*. Each strophe ends with a refrain (*efimnio*), which is usually identical in order to create poetic unity. Furthermore, the initial letters of each stanza spell the author's name (*acrostic*) and are often preceded by the adjective "humble". A prayer referring to the events celebrated or evoked concludes the hymn. After the biblical reading, Romanus sang the *Proemium*, usually in the form of a prayer or supplication. Thus he announced the topic of the sermon and explained the *refrain* to be repeated in chorus at the end of each stanza, which he delivered in rhythmic prose.

An important example is offered to us by the *kontakion* for Good Friday: it is a dramatic dialogue between Mary and her Son that takes place on the Way of the Cross. Mary says: "Where are you going, my Child? For whose sake are you finishing this swift race? I never thought I would see you, my Son, in such necessity, nor did I ever believe that the lawless would rage so and unjustly stretch out their hands against you"; Jesus answers: "Why, Mother, do you weep? . . . Lest I suffer? Lest I die? How then should I save Adam?" Mary's Son consoles his Mother, but reminds her of her role in the history of salvation: "Put aside your grief, Mother, put it aside; mourning is not right for you who have been called 'Full of Grace'" (*Mary at the Foot of the Cross* 1–2; 4–5). Then in the hymn on Abraham's sacrifice, Sarah claims for herself the decision on Isaac's life. Abraham says: "When Sarah hears, my Lord, all your words, upon knowing your will, she will say to me: If the one who has given it desires to repossess it, why did he give it? . . . O watchful one, leave me my son, and when he who called you wants him, it is to me that he must speak" (cf. *The Sacrifice of Abraham* 7).

Romanus used, not the solemn Byzantine Greek of the Imperial Court, but the simple Greek that was close to the language of the populace. I would like to cite here an example of the lively and highly personal manner in which he speaks about the Lord Jesus: he calls him the "source that is never consumed by fire and the light against the darkness" and says: "I long to hold you in my hand like a lamp; indeed, anyone who carries an oil lamp among men and women is illuminated without being burned. Illuminate me, then, you who are the light that never burns out" (*The Presentation* or *Feast of Encounter* 8). The force of conviction in his preaching was based on the close consistency between his words and his life. In one prayer he says: "Make my language clear, my Savior, open my mouth and, after filling it, penetrate my heart so that my acts may correspond to my words" (*Mission of the Apostles* 2).

Let us now examine some of his main themes. A fundamental subject that recurs in his preaching is the unity of God's action in history, the unity between Creation and the history of salvation, the unity between the Old and New Testaments. Another important theme is pneumatology, the teaching on the Holy Spirit. On the Feast of Pentecost, Romanus stressed the continuity that exists between Christ, ascended into Heaven, and the Apostles, that is, the Church, and he exalts missionary action in the world: "With divine virtue they conquered all men; they took up the Cross of Christ as a pen; they used words like 'fishing nets' and set them to 'catch' the world; they used the Word of God as a sharp hook, and as bait they used the flesh of the Sovereign One of the universe" (*Pentecost* 2:18).

Another central theme is, of course, Christology. Romanus did not involve himself in the difficult theological concepts, hotly debated at that time, which lacerated not only the unity of theologians but also the unity of Christians in the Church. He preached a simple but fundamental Christology, the Christology of the great Councils. Above all, however, Romanus was close to popular piety—moreover, the ideas of the Councils were inspired by popular piety and knowledge of the human heart—and in this way Romanus emphasized that Christ is true man and true God, and in being the true man-God, he is only one Person, the synthesis between Creation and the Creator, in whose human words we hear the voice of the Word of God himself. He said: "Christ was a man, but he was also God, yet he was not divided in two: He is One, the Son of a Father who is One alone" (*The Passion* 19). With regard to Mariology, grateful to the Virgin for his gift of a poetic talent, Romanus mentions her at the end of almost all his hymns and dedicated to her some of his most beautiful *kontakia*: *The Nativity of Christ, The Annunciation, The Divine Motherhood, The New Eve*.

Lastly, his moral teachings refer to the Last Judgment (*The Ten Virgins* [II]). He takes us toward this moment of truth in our lives, the appearance before the just Judge, and therefore exhorts us to conversion with penance and fasting. The positive aspect is that the Christian must practice charity and almsgiving. Romanus accentuated the primacy of charity over continence in two hymns—*The Wedding at Cana* and *The Ten Virgins*.

Charity is the greatest of the virtues: "Ten virgins possessed the virtue of virginity intact, but for five of them the difficult practice proved unfruitful. The others shone with their lamps of love for humanity, and for this reason the bridegroom invited them in" (*The Ten Virgins* 1). Vibrant humanity, the ardor of faith, and profound humility pervade the hymns of Romanus the Melodist. This great poet and composer reminds us of the whole treasure of Christian culture, born of faith, born of the heart that has encountered Christ, the Son of God. Culture, the whole of our great Christian culture, is born from this contact of the heart with the Truth who is Love. Nor, if faith stays alive, will this cultural inheritance die; rather, it will remain alive and present. To this day, images still speak to the hearts of believers; they are not relics of the past. Cathedrals are not medieval monuments but rather houses of life in which we feel "at home" and where we meet God and one another. Nor is great music—Gregorian chant, Bach, or Mozart—something of the past; rather, it lives on in the vitality of the liturgy and in our faith. If faith is alive, Christian culture can never become "obsolete" but, on the contrary, will remain alive and present. And if faith is alive, today, too, we can respond to the imperative that is ceaselessly repeated in the Psalms: "O Sing to the Lord a new song" (Ps 98[97]:1). Creativity, innovation, a new song, a new culture, and the presence of the entire cultural heritage are not mutually exclusive but form one reality: they are the presence of God's beauty and the joy of being his children.

6

Saint Gregory the Great (1)

WEDNESDAY, 28 MAY 2008
Saint Peter's Square

Dear Brothers and Sisters,

Last Wednesday I spoke of a Father of the Church little known in the West, Romanus the Melodist. Today I would like to present the figure of one of the greatest Fathers in the history of the Church, one of four Doctors of the West, Pope Saint Gregory, who was Bishop of Rome from 590 to 604 and who earned the traditional title of *Magnus/* the Great. Gregory was truly a great Pope and a great Doctor of the Church! He was born in Rome about 540 into a rich patrician family of the *gens Anicia*, who were distinguished not only for their noble blood but also for their adherence to the Christian faith and for their service to the Apostolic See. Two Popes came from this family: Felix III (483–492), the great-great grandfather of Gregory, and Agapetus (535–536). The house in which Gregory grew up stood on the Clivus Scauri, surrounded by majestic buildings that attested to the greatness of ancient Rome and the spiritual strength of Christianity. The example of his parents, Gordian and Sylvia, both venerated as Saints, and those of his father's sisters, Aemiliana and Tharsilla, who lived in their own home as consecrated virgins following a path of

37

prayer and self-denial, inspired lofty Christian sentiments
in him.

In the footsteps of his father, Gregory entered early into
an administrative career which reached its climax in 572,
when he became Prefect of the city. This office, complicated by the sorry times, allowed him to apply himself on
a vast range to every type of administrative problem, drawing light for future duties from them. In particular, he retained
a deep sense of order and discipline: having become Pope,
he advised Bishops to take as a model for the management
of ecclesial affairs diligence and respect for the law like civil
functionaries. Yet this life could not have satisfied him since,
shortly after, he decided to leave every civil assignment in
order to withdraw to his home to begin the monastic life,
transforming his family home into the monastery of Saint
Andrew on the Coelian Hill. This period of monastic life,
the life of permanent dialogue with the Lord in listening to
his Word, constituted a perennial nostalgia to which he
referred ever anew and ever more in his homilies. In the
midst of the pressure of pastoral worries, he often recalled
it in his writings as a happy time of recollection in God,
dedication to prayer, and peaceful immersion in study. Thus,
he could acquire that deep understanding of Sacred Scripture and of the Fathers of the Church that later served him
in his work.

But the cloistered withdrawal of Gregory did not last long.
The precious experience that he gained in civil adminis-
tration during a period marked by serious problems, the
relationships he had had in this post with the Byzantines,
and the universal respect that he acquired induced Pope
Pelagius to appoint him deacon and to send him to Constantinople as his "apocrisarius"—today one would say
"Apostolic Nuncio"—in order to help overcome the last

traces of the Monophysite controversy and above all to obtain
the Emperor's support in the effort to check the Lombard
invaders. The stay at Constantinople, where he resumed
monastic life with a group of monks, was very important
for Gregory, since it permitted him to acquire direct experience of the Byzantine world as well as to approach the
problem of the Lombards, who would later put his ability
and energy to the test during the years of his Pontificate.
After some years he was recalled to Rome by the Pope,
who appointed him his secretary. They were difficult years:
the continual rain, flooding due to overflowing rivers, the
famine that afflicted many regions of Italy as well as Rome.
Finally, even the plague broke out, which claimed numerous victims, among whom was also Pope Pelagius II. The
clergy, people, and senate were unanimous in choosing Gregory as his successor to the See of Peter. He tried to resist,
even attempting to flee, but to no avail: finally, he had to
yield. The year was 590.

Recognizing the will of God in what had happened, the
new Pontiff immediately and enthusiastically set to work.
From the beginning he showed a singularly enlightened vision
of the reality with which he had to deal, an extraordinary
capacity for work confronting both ecclesial and civil affairs,
a constant and even balance in making decisions, at times
with courage, imposed on him by his office.

Abundant documentation has been preserved from his governance thanks to the *Register* of his Letters (approximately
800), reflecting the complex questions that arrived on his
desk on a daily basis. They were questions that came from
Bishops, Abbots, clergy, and even from civil authorities of
every order and rank. Among the problems that afflicted Italy
and Rome at that time was one of special importance both
in the civil and ecclesial spheres: the Lombard question. The

Pope dedicated all possible energy to it in view of a truly peaceful solution. Contrary to the Byzantine Emperor, who assumed that the Lombards were only uncouth individuals and predators to be defeated or exterminated, Saint Gregory saw this people with the eyes of a good pastor and was concerned with proclaiming the word of salvation to them, establishing fraternal relationships with them in view of a future peace founded on mutual respect and peaceful coexistence between Italians, Imperials, and Lombards. He was concerned with the conversion of the young people and the new civil structure of Europe: the Visigoths of Spain, the Franks, the Saxons, the immigrants in Britain, and the Lombards were the privileged recipients of his evangelizing mission. Yesterday we celebrated the liturgical memorial of Saint Augustine of Canterbury, the leader of a group of monks Gregory assigned to go to Britain to evangelize England.

The Pope—who was a true peacemaker—deeply committed himself to establishing an effective peace in Rome and in Italy by undertaking intense negotiations with Agilulf, the Lombard King. This negotiation led to a period of truce that lasted for about three years (598–601), after which, in 603, it was possible to stipulate a more stable armistice. This positive result was obtained also thanks to the parallel contacts that, meanwhile, the Pope undertook with Queen Theodolinda, a Bavarian princess who, unlike the leaders of other Germanic peoples, was Catholic, deeply Catholic. A series of Letters of Pope Gregory to this Queen has been preserved in which he reveals his respect and friendship for her. Theodolinda, little by little, was able to guide the King to Catholicism, thus preparing the way to peace. The Pope also was careful to send her relics for the Basilica of Saint John the Baptist which she had had built in Monza and did not fail to send his congratulations and precious gifts for

the same Cathedral of Monza on the occasion of the birth
and baptism of her son, Adaloald. The series of events concerning this Queen constitutes a beautiful testimony to the
importance of women in the history of the Church. Gregory constantly focused on three basic objectives: to limit
the Lombard expansion in Italy; to preserve Queen Theodolinda from the influence of schismatics and to strengthen
the Catholic faith; and to mediate between the Lombards
and the Byzantines in view of an accord that guaranteed
peace in the Peninsula and at the same time permitted the
evangelization of the Lombards themselves. Therefore, in
the complex situation his focus was constantly twofold: to
promote understanding on the diplomatic-political level and
to spread the proclamation of the true faith among the
peoples.

Along with his purely spiritual and pastoral action, Pope
Gregory also became an active protagonist in multifaceted
social activities. With the revenues from the Roman See's
substantial patrimony in Italy, especially in Sicily, he bought
and distributed grain, assisted those in need, helped priests,
monks, and nuns who lived in poverty, paid the ransom for
citizens held captive by the Lombards, and purchased armistices
and truces. Moreover, whether in Rome or other parts of
Italy, he carefully carried out administrative reorganization,
giving precise instructions so that the goods of the Church,
useful for her sustenance and evangelizing work in the world,
were managed with absolute rectitude and according to the
rules of justice and mercy. He demanded that the tenants on
Church territory be protected from dishonest agents and, in
cases of fraud, quickly compensated, so that the face of the
Bride of Christ was not soiled with dishonest profits.

Gregory carried out this intense activity notwithstanding
his poor health, which often forced him to remain in bed

for days on end. The fasts practiced during the years of monastic life had caused him serious digestive problems. Furthermore, his voice was so feeble that he was often obliged to entrust the reading of his homilies to the deacon, so that the faithful present in the Roman Basilicas could hear him. On feast days he did his best to celebrate the *Missarum sollemnia*, that is, the solemn Mass, and then he met personally with the people of God, who were very fond of him, because they saw in him the authoritative reference from whom to draw security: not by chance was the title *consul Dei* quickly attributed to him. Notwithstanding the very difficult conditions in which he had to work, he gained the faithful's trust, thanks to his holiness of life and rich humanity, achieving truly magnificent results for his time and for the future. He was a man immersed in God: his desire for God was always alive in the depths of his soul, and precisely because of this he was always close to his neighbor, to the needy people of his time. Indeed, during a desperate period of havoc, he was able to create peace and give hope. This man of God shows us the true sources of peace, from which true hope comes. Thus, he becomes a guide also for us today.

7

Saint Gregory the Great (2)

Dear Brothers and Sisters,

Today, at our Wednesday appointment, I return to the extraordinary figure of Pope Gregory the Great to receive some additional light from his rich teaching. Notwithstanding the many duties connected to his office as the Bishop of Rome, he left to us numerous works, from which the Church in successive centuries has drawn with both hands. Besides the important correspondence—in last week's Catechesis I cited the *Register* that contains over eight hundred letters—first of all he left us writings of an exegetical character, among which his *Morals*, a commentary on Job (known under the Latin title *Moralia in Iob*), the *Homilies on Ezekiel*, and the *Homilies on the Gospel* stand out. Then there is an important work of a hagiographical character, the *Dialogues*, written by Gregory for the edification of the Lombard Queen Theodolinda. The primary and best-known work is undoubtedly the *Regula pastoralis* (*Pastoral Rule*), which the Pope published at the beginning of his Pontificate with clearly programmatic goals.

Wanting to review these works quickly, we must first of all note that, in his writings, Gregory never sought to delineate "his own" doctrine, his own originality. Rather, he intended to echo the traditional teaching of the Church; he simply wanted to be the mouthpiece of Christ and of the Church on the way that must be taken to reach God. His exegetical commentaries are models of this approach. He was a passionate reader of the Bible, which he approached not simply with a speculative purpose: from Sacred Scripture, he thought, the Christian must draw not theoretical understanding so much as the daily nourishment for his soul, for his life as man in this world. For example, in the *Homilies on Ezekiel*, he emphasized this function of the Sacred Text: to approach the Scripture simply to satisfy one's own desire for knowledge means to succumb to the temptation of pride and thus to expose oneself to the risk of sliding into heresy. Intellectual humility is the primary rule for one who seeks to penetrate the supernatural realities on the basis of the Sacred Book. Obviously, humility does not exclude serious study; but to ensure that the results are spiritually beneficial, facilitating true entry into the depth of the text, humility remains indispensable. Only with this interior attitude can one really listen to and eventually perceive the voice of God. On the other hand, when it is a question of the Word of God, understanding it means nothing if it does not lead to action. In these *Homilies on Ezekiel* is also found that beautiful expression according to which "the preacher must dip his pen into the blood of his heart; then he can also reach the ear of his neighbor." Reading his homilies, one sees that Gregory truly wrote with his life-blood, and, therefore, he still speaks to us today.

Gregory also developed this discourse in the *Book of Morals*, a commentary on Job. Following the Patristic tradition, he examined the Sacred Text in the three dimensions of its meaning: the literal dimension, the allegorical dimension, and the moral dimension, which are dimensions of the unique sense of Sacred Scripture. Nevertheless, Gregory gave a clear priority to the moral sense. In this perspective, he proposed his thought by way of some expressive pairs of words—*know–do, speak–live, know–act*—in which he evokes the two aspects of human life that should be complementary but which often end by being antithetical. The moral ideal, he comments, always consists in realizing a harmonious integration between word and action, thought and deed, prayer and dedication to the duties of one's state: this is the way to realize that synthesis thanks to which the divine descends to man and man is lifted up until he becomes one with God. Thus the great Pope marks out a complete plan of life for the authentic believer; for this reason the *Book of Morals*, a commentary on Job, would constitute in the course of the Middle Ages a kind of *summa* of Christian morality.

Of notable importance and beauty are also the *Homilies on the Gospel*. The first of these was given in Saint Peter's Basilica in 590 during the Advent Season, hence only a few months after Gregory's election to the Papacy; the last was delivered in Saint Lawrence's Basilica on the Second Sunday after Pentecost in 593. The Pope preached to the people in the churches where the "stations" were celebrated—special prayer ceremonies during the important seasons of the liturgical year—or the feasts of titular martyrs. The guiding principle, which links the different homilies, is captured in the word "*preacher*": not only the minister of God, but also every Christian has the duty "to preach" of what he has experienced in his innermost being, following the example of Christ, who was made man to bring to all the good news of salvation. The horizon of this commitment is eschatological: the expectation of the fulfillment of all things in Christ was a constant thought of the great Pontiff and ended by becoming the motive that inspired his every thought and activity. From

here sprang his incessant reminders to be vigilant and to per-
form good works.

Probably the most organic text of Gregory the Great is
the *Pastoral Rule*, written in the first years of his Pontificate.
In it Gregory proposed to treat the figure of the ideal Bishop,
the teacher and guide of his flock. To this end he illustrated
the seriousness of the office of pastor of the Church and its
inherent duties. Therefore, those who were not called to
this office may not seek it with superficiality; instead, those
who assumed it without due reflection necessarily feel a
proper trepidation rise within their soul. Taking up again a
favorite theme, he affirmed that the Bishop is above all the
"preacher" par excellence; for this reason he must be above
all an example for others, so that his behavior may be a
point of reference for all. Efficacious pastoral action requires
that he know his audience and adapt his words to the situation of each person: here Gregory paused to illustrate the
various categories of the faithful with acute and precise anno-
tations, which can justify the evaluation of those who have
also seen in this work a treatise on psychology. From this
one understands that he really knew his flock and spoke of
all things with the people of his time and his city.

Nevertheless, the great Pontiff insisted on the pastor's duty
to recognize daily his own unworthiness in the eyes of the
Supreme Judge, so that pride did not negate the good accomplished. For this reason the final chapter of the *Rule* is dedicated to humility: "When one is pleased to have achieved
many virtues, it is well to reflect on one's own inadequacies
and to humble oneself: instead of considering the good
accomplished, it is necessary to consider what was neglected."
All these precious indications demonstrate the lofty concept that Saint Gregory had for the care of souls, which he
defined as the "*ars artium*", the art of arts. The *Rule* had

such great, and the rather rare, good fortune to have been quickly translated into Greek and Anglo-Saxon.

Another significant work is the *Dialogues*. In this work addressed to his friend Peter, the deacon, who was convinced that customs were so corrupt as to impede the rise of Saints as in times past, Gregory demonstrated just the opposite: holiness is always possible, even in difficult times. He proved it by narrating the life of contemporaries or those who had died recently, who could well be considered Saints, even if not canonized. The narration was accompanied by theological and mystical reflections that make the book a singular hagiographical text, capable of enchanting entire generations of readers. The material was drawn from the living traditions of the people and intended to edify and form, attracting the attention of the reader to a series of questions regarding the meaning of miracles, the interpretation of Scripture, the immortality of the soul, the existence of Hell, the representation of the next world—all themes that require fitting clarification. Book II is wholly dedicated to the figure of Benedict of Norcia and is the only ancient witness to the life of the holy monk, whose spiritual beauty the text highlights fully.

In the theological plan that Gregory develops regarding his works, the past, present, and future are compared. What counted for him more than anything was the entire arc of salvation history, which continues to unfold in the obscure meanderings of time. In this perspective it is significant that he inserted the news of the conversion of the Angles in the middle of his *Book of Morals*, a commentary on Job: to his eyes the event constituted a furthering of the Kingdom of God which the Scripture treats. Therefore, it could rightly be mentioned in the commentary on a holy book. According to him, the leaders of Christian communities must commit themselves to rereading events in the light of the Word of God: in this sense the great Pontiff felt he had the duty to orient pastors and the faithful on the spiritual itinerary of an enlightened and correct *lectio divina*, placed in the context of one's own life.

Before concluding, it is necessary to say a word on the relationship that Pope Gregory nurtured with the Patriarchs of Antioch, of Alexandria, and of Constantinople itself. He always concerned himself with recognizing and respecting rights, protecting them from every interference that would limit legitimate autonomy. Still, if Saint Gregory, in the context of the historical situation, was opposed to the title "ecumenical" on the part of the Patriarch of Constantinople, it was not to limit or negate this legitimate authority but rather because he was concerned about the fraternal unity of the universal Church. Above all he was profoundly convinced that humility should be the fundamental virtue for every Bishop, even more so for the Patriarch. Gregory remained a simple monk in his heart and therefore was decidedly opposed to great titles. He wanted to be—and this is his expression—*servus servorum Dei*. Coined by him, this phrase was not just a pious formula on his lips but a true manifestation of his way of living and acting. He was intimately struck by the humility of God, who in Christ made himself our servant. He washed and washes our dirty feet. Therefore, he was convinced that a Bishop, above all, should imitate this humility of God and follow Christ in this way. His desire was to live truly as a monk, in permanent contact with the Word of God, but for love of God he knew how to make himself the servant of all in a time full of tribulation and suffering. He knew how to make himself the "servant of the servants". Precisely because he was this, he is great and also shows us the measure of true greatness.

8

Saint Columban

Dear Brothers and Sisters,

Today I would like to speak about the holy Abbot Columban, the best-known Irishman of the early Middle Ages. Since he worked as a monk, missionary, and writer in various countries of Western Europe, with good reason he can be called a "European" Saint. With the Irish of his time, he had a sense of Europe's cultural unity. The expression "*totius Europae*—of all Europe", with reference to the Church's presence on the Continent, is found for the first time in one of his letters, written around the year 600, addressed to Pope Gregory the Great (cf. *Epistula* I, 1).

Columban was born *ca.* 543 in the Province of Leinster in southeast Ireland. He was educated at home by excellent tutors who introduced him to the study of liberal arts. He was then entrusted to the guidance of Abbot Sinell of the community of Cleenish in Northern Ireland, where he was able to deepen his study of Sacred Scripture. At the age of about twenty, he entered the monastery of Bangor, in the northeast of the island, whose Abbot, Comgall, was a monk well known for his virtue and ascetic rigor. In full agreement with his Abbot, Columban zealously practiced the severe discipline of the monastery, leading a life of prayer, ascesis, and study. While there, he was also ordained a priest. His life at Bangor and the Abbot's example influenced the conception of monasticism that developed in Columban over time and that he subsequently spread in the course of his life.

When he was approximately fifty years old, following the characteristically Irish ascetic ideal of the *"peregrinatio pro Christo"*, namely, making oneself a pilgrim for the sake of Christ, Columban left his island with twelve companions to engage in missionary work on the European Continent. We should in fact bear in mind that the migration of people from the North and the East had caused whole areas, previously Christianized, to revert to paganism. Around the year 590, the small group of missionaries landed on the Breton coast. Welcomed kindly by the King of the Franks of Austrasia (present-day France), they asked only for a small piece of uncultivated land. They were given the ancient Roman fortress of Annegray, totally ruined and abandoned and covered by forest. Accustomed to a life of extreme hardship, in the span of a few months the monks managed to build the first hermitage on the ruins. Thus their re-evangelization began, in the first place, through the witness of their lives. With the new cultivation of the land, they also began a new cultivation of souls. The fame of those foreign religious who, living on prayer and in great austerity, built houses and worked the land spread rapidly, attracting pilgrims and penitents. In particular, many young men asked to be accepted by the monastic community in order to live, like them, this exemplary life which was renewing the cultivation of the land and of souls. It was not long before the foundation of a second monastery was required. It was built a few kilometers away on the ruins of an ancient spa, Luxeuil. This monastery was to become the center of the traditional Irish monastic and missionary outreach on the European Continent. A third monastery was erected at Fontaine, an hour's walk further north.

Columban lived at Luxeuil for almost twenty years. Here the Saint wrote for his followers the *Regula monachorum*— for a while more widespread in Europe than Benedict's *Rule*—which portrayed the ideal image of the monk. It is the only ancient Irish monastic rule in our possession today. Columban integrated it with the *Regula coenobialis*, a sort of penal code for the offenses committed by monks, with punishments that are somewhat surprising to our modern sensibility and can only be explained by the mentality and environment of that time. With another famous work entitled: *De poenitentiarum misura taxanda*, also written at Luxeuil, Columban introduced Confession and private and frequent penance on the Continent. It was known as "tariffed" penance because of the proportion established between the gravity of the sin and the type of penance imposed by the confessor. These innovations roused the suspicion of local Bishops, a suspicion that became hostile when Columban had the courage to rebuke them openly for the practices of some of them. The controversy over the date of Easter was an opportunity to demonstrate their opposition: Ireland, in fact, followed the Eastern rather than the Roman tradition. The Irish monk was summoned in 603 to account to a Synod at Chalon-sur-Saône for his practices regarding penance and Easter. Instead of presenting himself before the Synod, he sent a letter in which he minimized the issue, inviting the Synod Fathers not only to discuss the problem of the date of Easter, in his opinion a negligible problem, "but also all the necessary canonical norms that—something more serious—are disregarded by many" (cf. *Epistula* II, 1). At the same time he wrote to

Pope Boniface IV—just as several years earlier he had turned to Pope Gregory the Great (cf. *Epistula* I)—asking him to defend the Irish tradition (cf. *Epistula* III).

Intransigent as he was in every moral matter, Columban then came into conflict with the royal house for having harshly reprimanded King Theuderic for his adulterous relations. This created a whole network of personal, religious, and political intrigues and maneuvers which, in 610, culminated in a Decree of expulsion banishing Columban and all the monks of Irish origin from Luxeuil and condemning them to definitive exile. They were escorted to the sea and, at the expense of the court, boarded a ship bound for Ireland. However, not far from shore the ship ran aground, and the captain, who saw this as a sign from Heaven, abandoned the voyage and, for fear of being cursed by God, brought the monks back to dry land. Instead of returning to Luxeuil, they decided to begin a new work of evangelization. Thus, they embarked on a Rhine boat and traveled up the river. After a first stop in Tuggen near Lake Zurich, they went to the region of Bregenz, near Lake Constance, to evangelize the Alemanni.

However, soon afterward, because of political events unfavorable to his work, Columban decided to cross the Alps with the majority of his disciples. Only one monk, whose name was Gallus, stayed behind; it was from his hermitage that the famous Abbey of Saint Gall in Switzerland subsequently developed. Having arrived in Italy, Columban met with a warm welcome at the Lombard Royal Court but was immediately faced with considerable difficulties: the life of the Church was torn apart by the Arian heresy, still prevalent among the Lombards, and by a schism which had detached most of the Church in Northern Italy from communion with the Bishop of Rome. Columban entered authoritatively into this context, writing a satirical pamphlet against Arianism and a letter to Boniface IV to convince him to take some decisive steps with a view to re-establishing unity (cf. *Epistula* V). When, in 612 or 613, the King of the Lombards allocated to him a plot of land in Bobbio, in the Trebbia Valley, Columban founded a new monastery there which was later to become a cultural center on a par with the famous monastery of Monte Cassino. Here he came to the end of his days: he died on 23 November 615 and to this day is commemorated on this date in the Roman rite.

Saint Columban's message is concentrated in a firm appeal to conversion and detachment from earthly goods, with a view to the eternal inheritance. With his ascetic life and conduct free from compromises when he faced the corruption of the powerful, he is reminiscent of the severe figure of Saint John the Baptist. His austerity, however, was never an end in itself but merely the means with which to open himself freely to God's love and to correspond with his whole being to the gifts received from him, thereby restoring in himself the image of God, while at the same time cultivating the earth and renewing human society. I quote from his *Instructiones*: "If man makes a correct use of those faculties that God has conceded to his soul, he will be likened to God. Let us remember that we must restore to him all those gifts which he deposited in us when we were in our original condition. He has taught us the way with his Commandments. The first of them tells us to love the Lord with all our heart, because he loved us first, from the beginning of time, even before we came into the light of this world" (cf. *Instructiones* XI). The Irish Saint truly incarnated these words in his own life. A man of great culture—he also wrote poetry in Latin and a grammar book—he proved rich in gifts of grace. He was a tireless builder of monasteries as well as an intransigent penitential preacher who spent every ounce of his energy on nurturing the Christian roots of Europe, which was coming into existence. With his spiritual energy, with his faith, with his love for God and neighbor, he truly became one of the Fathers of Europe. He shows us even today the roots from which our Europe can be reborn.

9

Saint Isidore of Seville

WEDNESDAY, 18 JUNE 2008
Saint Peter's Square

Dear Brothers and Sisters,

Today I would like to speak about Saint Isidore of Seville. He was a younger brother of Leander, Archbishop of Seville, and a great friend of Pope Gregory the Great. Pointing this out is important because it enables us to bear in mind a cultural and spiritual approach that is indispensable for understanding Isidore's personality. Indeed, he owed much to Leander, an exacting, studious, and austere person who created around his younger brother a family environment marked by the ascetic requirements proper to a monk and by a rhythm of work demanded by a serious dedication to study. Furthermore, Leander was concerned to prepare what was necessary to confront the political and social situation of that time: in those decades, in fact, the Visigoths, barbarians and Arians, had invaded the Iberian Peninsula and taken possession of territories that belonged to the Roman Empire. It was essential to regain them for the Roman world and for Catholicism. Leander and Isidore's home was furnished with a library richly endowed with classical pagan and Christian works. Isidore, who felt simultaneously attracted to both, was therefore taught under the stewardship of his elder

55

brother to develop a very strong discipline, in devoting himself to study them with discretion and discernment.

Thus a calm and open atmosphere prevailed in the episcopal residence in Seville. We can deduce this from Isidore's cultural and spiritual interests, as they emerge from his works themselves, which include an encyclopedic knowledge of pagan classical culture and a thorough knowledge of Christian culture. This explains the eclecticism characteristic of Isidore's literary opus, which glided with the greatest of ease from Martial to Augustine or from Cicero to Gregory the Great. The inner strife that the young Isidore had to contend with, having succeeded his brother Leander on the episcopal throne of Seville in 599, was by no means unimportant. The impression of excessive voluntarism that strikes one on reading the works of this great author, considered to be the last of the Christian Fathers of antiquity, may, perhaps, actually be due to this constant struggle with himself. A few years after his death in 636, the Council of Toledo in 653 described him as "an illustrious teacher of our time and the glory of the Catholic Church".

Isidore was without a doubt a man of marked dialectic antitheses. Moreover, he experienced a permanent inner conflict in his personal life, similar to that which Gregory the Great and Saint Augustine had experienced earlier, between a desire for solitude to dedicate himself solely to meditation on the Word of God and the demands of charity to his brethren, for whose salvation, as Bishop, he felt responsible. He wrote, for example, with regard to Church leaders: "*The man responsible for a Church (vir ecclesiasticus)* must, on the one hand, allow himself to be crucified to the world with the mortification of his flesh and, on the other, accept the decision of the ecclesiastical order—when it comes from God's will—to devote himself humbly to government, even if he does not wish to" (*Sententiarum liber* III, 33, 1: *PL* 83, 705 B). Just a paragraph later he adds:

Men of God (*sancti viri*) do not in fact desire to dedicate themselves to things of the world and groan when by some mysterious design of God they are charged with certain responsibilities. . . . They do their utmost to avoid them but accept what they would like to shun and do what they would have preferred to avoid. Indeed, they enter into the secrecy of the heart and seek there to understand what God's mysterious will is asking of them. And when they realize that they must submit to God's plans, they bend their hearts to the yoke of the divine decision. (*Sententiarum liber* III, 33, 3: *PL* 83, 705–706)

To understand Isidore better it is first of all necessary to recall the complexity of the political situations in his time to which I have already referred: during the years of his boyhood he was obliged to experience the bitterness of exile. He was nevertheless pervaded with apostolic enthusiasm. He experienced the rapture of contributing to the formation of a people that was at last rediscovering its unity, both political and religious, with the providential conversion of Hermenegild, the heir to the Visigoth throne, from Arianism to the Catholic faith. Yet we must not underestimate the enormous difficulty of coming to grips with such very serious problems as the relations with heretics and with the Jews. There was a whole series of problems which appear very concrete to us today, too, especially if we consider what is happening in certain regions in which we seem almost to be witnessing the recurrence of situations very similar to those that existed on the Iberian Peninsula in that sixth century. The wealth of cultural knowledge that Isidore had assimilated enabled him constantly to compare the Christian newness with the

Greco-Roman cultural heritage; however, rather than the precious gift of synthesis, it would seem that he possessed the gift of *collatio*, that is, of collecting, which he expressed in an extraordinary personal erudition, although it was not always ordered as might have been desired.

In any case, his deep concern not to overlook anything that human experience had produced in the history of his homeland and of the whole world is admirable. Isidore did not want to lose anything that man had acquired in the epochs of antiquity, regardless of whether they had been pagan, Jewish, or Christian. Hence, it should not come as a surprise if, in pursuing this goal, he did not always manage to filter the knowledge he possessed sufficiently through the purifying waters of the Christian faith as he would have wished. The point is, however, that in Isidore's intentions, the proposals he made were always in tune with the Catholic faith which he staunchly upheld. In the discussion of the various theological problems, he showed that he perceived their complexity and often astutely suggested solutions that summarize and express the complete Christian truth. This has enabled believers through the ages and to our times to profit with gratitude from his definitions. A significant example of this is offered by Isidore's teaching on the relations between active and contemplative life. He wrote: "Those who seek to attain repose in contemplation must first train in the stadium of active life; and then, free from the dross of sin, they will be able to display that pure heart which alone makes the vision of God possible" (*Differentiarum Lib. II*, 34, 133: *PL* 83, 91A). Nonetheless, the realism of a true pastor convinced him of the risk the faithful run of reducing themselves to one dimension. He therefore added: "The middle way, consisting of both of these forms of life, normally turns out to be more useful in resolving those tensions which are often aggravated by the choice of a single way of life and are instead better tempered by an alternation of the two forms" (*op. cit.*, 134; *ibid.*, col. 91B).

Isidore sought in Christ's example the definitive confirmation of a just orientation of life and said: "The Savior Jesus offers us the example of active life when during the day he devoted himself to working signs and miracles in the town, but he showed the contemplative life when he withdrew to the mountain and spent the night in prayer" (*op. cit.*, 134: *ibid.*). In the light of this example of the divine Teacher, Isidore can conclude with this precise moral teaching: "Therefore let the servant of God, imitating Christ, dedicate himself to contemplation without denying himself active life. Behaving otherwise would not be right. Indeed, just as we must love God in contemplation, so we must love our neighbor with action. It is therefore impossible to live without the presence of both the one and the other form of life, nor can we live without experiencing both the one and the other" (*op. cit.*, 135; *ibid.*, 91C). I consider that this is the synthesis of a life that seeks contemplation of God, dialogue with God in prayer and in the reading of Sacred Scripture, as well as action at the service of the human community and of our neighbor. This synthesis is the lesson that the great Bishop of Seville has bequeathed to us, Christians of today, called to witness to Christ at the beginning of a new millennium.

10

Saint Maximus the Confessor

Dear Brothers and Sisters,

Today I would like to present the figure of one of the great Fathers of the Eastern Church in later times. He is a monk, Saint Maximus, whose fearless courage in witnessing to—"confessing"—even while suffering, the integrity of his faith in Jesus Christ, true God and true man, Savior of the world, earned him Christian tradition's title of *Confessor*. Maximus was born in Palestine, the land of the Lord, in about 580. As a boy he was initiated into the monastic life and the study of the Scriptures through the works of Origen, the great teacher who by the third century had already "established" the exegetic tradition of Alexandria.

Maximus moved from Jerusalem to Constantinople and from there, because of the barbarian invasions, sought refuge in Africa. Here he was distinguished by his extreme courage in the defense of orthodoxy. Maximus refused to accept any reduction of Christ's humanity. A theory had come into being which held that there was only one will in Christ, the divine will. To defend the oneness of Christ's Person, people denied that he had his own true and proper human will. And, at first sight, it might seem to be a good thing that

Christ had only one will. But Saint Maximus immediately realized that this would destroy the mystery of salvation, for humanity without a will, a man without a will, is not a real man but an amputated man. Had this been so, the man Jesus Christ would not have been a true man, he would not have experienced the drama of being human, which consists, precisely, of conforming our will with the great truth of being. Thus Saint Maximus declared with great determination: Sacred Scripture does not portray to us an amputated man with no will but rather true and complete man: God, in Jesus Christ, really assumed the totality of being human—obviously with the exception of sin—hence also a human will. And said like this, his point is clear: Christ either is or is not a man. If he is a man, he also has a will. But here the problem arises: do we not end up with a sort of dualism? Do we not reach the point of affirming two complete personalities: reason, will, sentiment? How is it possible to overcome dualism, to keep the completeness of the human being and yet succeed in preserving the unity of the Person of Christ, who was not schizophrenic? Saint Maximus demonstrates that man does not find his unity, the integration of himself or his totality, within himself but by surpassing himself, by coming out of himself. Thus, also in Christ, by coming out of himself, man finds himself in God, in the Son of God. It is not necessary to amputate man to explain the Incarnation; all that is required is to understand the dynamism of the human being who is fulfilled only by coming out of himself; it is in God alone that we find ourselves, our totality and our completeness. Hence, we see that the person who withdraws into himself is not a complete person, but the person who is open, who comes out of himself, becomes complete and finds himself, finds his true humanity, precisely in the Son of God. For Saint Maximus, this vision did not remain a philosophical speculation; he saw it realized in Jesus' actual life, especially in the drama of Gethsemane. In this drama of Jesus' agony, of the anguish of death, of the opposition between the human will not to die and the divine will which offers itself to death, in this drama of Gethsemane the whole human drama is played out, the drama of our redemption. Saint Maximus tells us that, and we know that this is true, Adam (and we ourselves are Adam) thought that the "no" was the peak of freedom. He thought that only a person who can say "no" is truly free; that if he is truly to achieve his freedom, man must say "no" to God; only in this way, he believed, could he at last be himself, could he reach the heights of freedom. The human nature of Christ also carried this tendency within it but overcame it, for Jesus saw that it was not the "no" that was the height of freedom. The height of freedom is the "yes", in conformity with God's will. It is only in the "yes" that man truly becomes himself; only in the great openness of the "yes", in the unification of his will with the divine, that man becomes immensely open, becomes "divine". What Adam wanted was to be like God, that is, to be completely free. But the person who withdraws into himself is not divine, is not completely free; he is freed by emerging from himself, it is in the "yes" that he becomes free; and this is the drama of Gethsemane: not my will but yours. It is by transferring the human will to the divine will that the real person is born; it is in this way that we are redeemed. This, in a few brief words, is the fundamental point of what Saint Maximus wanted to say, and here we see that the whole human being is truly at issue; the entire question of our life lies here. In Africa Saint Maximus was already having problems defending this vision of man and of God. He was then summoned to Rome. In 649 he took an active part in the Lateran Council, convoked by Pope Martin I to defend the two wills of Christ against the Imperial Edict which—*pro bono pacis*—forbade discussion of this matter. Pope Martin was made to pay dearly for his courage. Although he was in a precarious state of health, he was arrested and taken to Constantinople. Tried and condemned to death, the Pope obtained the commutation of his sentence to permanent exile in the Crimea, where he died on 16 September 655, after two long years of humiliation and torment.

It was Maximus' turn shortly afterward, in 662, as he too opposed the Emperor, repeating: "It cannot be said that Christ has a single will!" (cf. *PG* 91, 268–269). Thus, together with his two disciples, both called Anastasius, Maximus was subjected to an exhausting trial although he was then over eighty years of age. The Emperor's tribunal condemned him with the accusation of heresy, sentencing him to the cruel mutilation of his tongue and his right hand—the two organs through which, by words and writing, Maximus had fought the erroneous doctrine of the single will of Christ. In the end, thus mutilated, the holy monk was finally exiled to the region of Colchis on the Black Sea, where he died, worn out by the suffering he had endured, at the age of eighty-two, on 13 August that same year, 662.

In speaking of Maximus' life, we mentioned his literary opus in defense of orthodoxy. We referred in particular to the *Disputation with Pyrrhus*, formerly Patriarch of Constantinople: in this debate he succeeded in persuading his adversary of his errors. With great honesty, in fact, Pyrrhus concluded the *Disputation* with these words: "I ask forgiveness for myself and for those who have preceded me: by ignorance we arrived at these absurd ideas and arguments; and I ask that a way may be found to cancel these absurdities, saving the memory of those who erred" (*PG* 91, 352). Also several dozen important works have been handed down to us, among which the *Mystagogia* is outstanding. This is one of Saint Maximus' most important writings, which gathers his theological thought in a well-structured synthesis.

Saint Maximus' thought was never merely theological, speculative, or introverted because its target was always the practical reality of the world and its salvation. In this context in which he had to suffer, he could not escape into purely theoretical and philosophical affirmations. He had to seek the meaning of life, asking himself: who am I? What is the world? God entrusted to man, created in his image and likeness, the mission of unifying the cosmos. And just as Christ unified the human being in himself, the Creator unified the cosmos in man. He showed us how to unify the cosmos in the communion of Christ and thus truly arrived at a redeemed world. Hans Urs von Balthasar, one of the greatest theologians of the twentieth century, referred to this powerful saving vision when—"relaunching" Maximus—he defined his thought with the vivid expression *Kosmische Liturgie*, "cosmic liturgy". Jesus, the one Savior of the world, is always at the center of this solemn "liturgy". The efficacy of his saving action, which definitively unified the cosmos, is guaranteed by the fact that in spite of being God in all things, he is also integrally a man and has the "energy" and will of a man.

The life and thought of Maximus were powerfully illumined by his immense courage in witnessing to the integral reality of Christ, without any reduction or compromise. And thus it becomes clear who man really is and how we should live in order to respond to our vocation. We must live united to God in order to be united to ourselves and to the cosmos, giving the cosmos itself and humanity their proper form. Christ's universal "yes" also shows us clearly how to put all the other values in the right place. We think of values that are justly defended today, such as tolerance, freedom, and dialogue. But a tolerance that no longer distinguishes between good and evil would become chaotic and self-destructive, just as a freedom that did not respect the freedom of others or find the common measure of our respective liberties would become anarchy and destroy authority. Dialogue that no longer knows what to discuss becomes empty chatter. All these values are important and fundamental but can remain true values only if they have the point of reference that unites them and gives them true authenticity. This reference point is the synthesis between God and the cosmos, the figure of Christ in which we learn the truth about ourselves and thus where to rank all other values, because we discover their authentic meaning. Jesus Christ is the reference point that gives light to all other values. This was the conclusion of the great Confessor's witness. And it is in this way, ultimately, that Christ indicates that the cosmos must become a liturgy, the glory of God, and that worship is the beginning of the true transformation, of the true renewal of the world.

I would therefore like to conclude with a fundamental passage from one of Saint Maximus' works: "We adore one Son together with the Father and the Holy Spirit, as it was in the beginning before all time, is now, and ever shall be, for all time and for the time after time. Amen!" (PG 91, 269).

11

John Climacus

WEDNESDAY, 11 FEBRUARY 2009
Paul VI Audience Hall

Dear Brothers and Sisters,

After twenty Catecheses dedicated to the Apostle Paul, today I would like to return to presenting the great writers of the Church of the East and of the West in the Middle Ages. And I am proposing the figure of John known as Climacus, a Latin transliteration of the Greek term *klimakos*, which means *of the ladder* (*klimax*). This is the title of his most important work, in which he describes the ladder of human life ascending toward God. He was born in about 575 A.D. He lived, therefore, during the years in which Byzantium, the capital of the Roman Empire of the East, experienced the greatest crisis in its history. The geographical situation of the Empire suddenly changed, and the torrent of barbarian invasions swept away all its structures. Only the structure of the Church withstood them, continuing in these difficult times to carry out her missionary, human, social, and cultural action, especially through the network of monasteries in which great religious figures such as, precisely, John Climacus were active.

John lived and told of his spiritual experiences in the mountains of Sinai, where Moses encountered God and Elijah heard his voice. Information on him has been preserved in a brief *Life* (*PG* 88, 596–608), written by a monk, Daniel of Raithu. At the age of sixteen, John, who had become a monk on Mount Sinai, made himself a disciple of Abba Martyrius, an "elder", that is, a "wise man". At about twenty years of age, he chose to live as a hermit in a grotto at the foot of the mountain in the locality of Tola, eight kilometers from the present-day Saint Catherine's Monastery. Solitude, however, did not prevent him from meeting people eager for spiritual direction or from paying visits to several monasteries near Alexandria. In fact, far from being an escape from the world and human reality, his eremitical retreat led to ardent love for others (*Life*, 5) and for God (*ibid.*, 7). After forty years of life as a hermit, lived in love for God and for neighbor, years in which he wept, prayed, and fought with demons, he was appointed hegumen of the large monastery on Mount Sinai and thus returned to cenobitic life in a monastery. However, several years before his death, nostalgic for the eremitical life, he handed over the government of the community to his brother, a monk in the same monastery. John died after the year 650. He lived his life between two mountains, Sinai and Tabor, and one can truly say that he radiated the light which Moses saw on Sinai and which was contemplated by the three Apostles on Mount Tabor!

He became famous, as I have already said, through his work entitled *The Ladder* (*klimax*), in the West known as the *Ladder of Divine Ascent* (*PG* 88, 632–1164). Composed at the insistent request of the hegumen of the neighboring Monastery of Raithu in Sinai, the *Ladder* is a complete treatise of the spiritual life in which John describes the monk's journey from renunciation of the world to the perfection of love. This journey—according to his book—covers thirty steps, each one of which is linked to the next. The journey may be summarized in three consecutive stages: the first is expressed in renunciation of the world in order to return to a state of evangelical childhood. Thus, the essential is not the renunciation but rather the connection with what Jesus said, that is, the return to true childhood in the spiritual sense, becoming like children. John comments: "A good foundation of three layers and three pillars is: innocence, fasting, and temperance. Let all babes in Christ (cf. 1 Cor 3:1) begin with these virtues, taking as their model the natural babes" (1, 20; 636). Voluntary detachment from beloved people and places permits the soul to enter into deeper communion with God. This renunciation leads to obedience, which is the way to humility through humiliations—which will never be absent—on the part of the brethren. John comments: "Blessed is he who has mortified his will to the very end and has entrusted the care of himself to his teacher in the Lord: indeed, he will be placed on the right hand of the Crucified One!" (4, 37; 704).

The second stage of the journey consists in spiritual combat against the passions. Every step of the ladder is linked to a principal passion that is defined and diagnosed, with an indication of the treatment and a proposal of the corresponding virtue. All together, these steps of the ladder undoubtedly constitute the most important treatise of spiritual strategy that we possess. The struggle against the passions, however, is steeped in the positive—it does not remain as something negative—thanks to the image of the "fire" of the Holy Spirit: that "all those who enter upon the good fight (cf. 1 Tm 6:12), which is hard and narrow, ... may realize that they must leap into the fire, if they really expect the celestial fire to dwell in them" (1, 18; 636). The fire of the Holy Spirit is the fire of love and truth. The power of the Holy Spirit alone guarantees victory.

However, according to John Climacus it is important to be aware that the passions are not evil in themselves; they become so through human freedom's wrong use of them. If they are purified, the passions reveal to man the path toward God with energy unified by ascesis and grace, and, "if they have received from the Creator an order and a beginning . . . , the limit of virtue is boundless" (26/2, 37; 1068).

The last stage of the journey is Christian perfection, which is developed in the last seven steps of the *Ladder*. These are the highest stages of spiritual life, which can be experienced by the "Hesychasts": the solitaries, those who have attained quiet and inner peace; but these stages are also accessible to the more fervent cenobites. Of the first three— simplicity, humility, and discernment—John, in line with the Desert Fathers, considered the ability to discern the most important. Every type of behavior must be subject to discernment; everything, in fact, depends on one's deepest motivations, which need to be closely examined. Here one enters into the soul of the person, and it is a question of reawakening in the hermit, in the Christian, spiritual sensitivity and a "feeling heart", which are gifts from God: "After God, we ought to follow our conscience as a rule and guide in everything" (26/1, 5; 1013). In this way one reaches tranquility of soul, *hesychia*, by means of which the soul may gaze upon the abyss of the divine mysteries.

The state of quiet, of inner peace, prepares the Hesychast for prayer, which in John is twofold: "corporeal prayer" and "prayer of the heart". The former is proper to those who need the help of bodily movement: stretching out the hands, uttering groans, beating the breast, etc. (15, 26; 900). The latter is spontaneous, because it is an effect of the reawakening of spiritual sensitivity, a gift of God to those who devote

themselves to corporeal prayer. In John this takes the name
"Jesus prayer" (*Iesoû euché*) and is constituted in the invocation solely of Jesus' name, an invocation that is continuous
like breathing: "May your remembrance of Jesus become one
with your breathing, and you will then know the usefulness
of *hesychia*", inner peace (27/2, 26; 1112). At the end, the
prayer becomes very simple: the word "Jesus" simply becomes
one with the breath.

   The last step of the ladder (30), suffused with "the sober
inebriation of the spirit", is dedicated to the supreme "trinity of virtues": faith, hope, and above all charity. John also
speaks of charity as *eros* (human love), a symbol of the mat-
rimonial union of the soul with God, and once again chooses
the image of fire to express the fervor, light, and purification of love for God. The power of human love can be
reoriented to God, just as a cultivated olive may be grafted
on to a wild olive tree (cf. Rm 11:24) (cf. 15, 66; 893).
John is convinced that an intense experience of this *eros*
will help the soul to advance far more than the harsh struggle against the passions, because of its great power. Thus, in
our journey, the positive aspect prevails. Yet charity is also
seen in close relation to hope: "Hope is the power that
drives love. Thanks to hope, we can look forward to the
reward of charity. . . . Hope is the doorway of love. . . . The
absence of hope destroys charity: our efforts are bound to
it, our labors are sustained by it, and through it we are
enveloped by the mercy of God" (30, 16; 1157). The conclusion of the *Ladder* contains the synthesis of the work in
words that the author has God himself utter: "May this ladder teach you the spiritual disposition of the virtues. I am
at the summit of the ladder, and as my great initiate (Saint
Paul) said: '*So faith, hope, love abide, these three; but the greatest
of these is love*' (1 Cor 13:13)!" (30, 18; 1160).

At this point, a last question must be asked: can the *Ladder*, a work written by a hermit monk who lived 1,400 years ago, say something to us today? Can the existential journey of a man who lived his entire life on Mount Sinai in such a distant time be relevant to us? At first glance it would seem that the answer must be "no", because John Climacus is too remote from us. But if we look a little closer, we see that the monastic life is only a great symbol of baptismal life, of Christian life. It shows, so to speak, in capital letters what we write day after day in small letters. It is a prophetic symbol that reveals what the life of the baptized person is, in communion with Christ, with his death and Resurrection. The fact that the top of the "ladder", the final steps, are at the same time the fundamental, initial, and most simple virtues is particularly important to me: faith, hope, and charity. These are not virtues accessible only to moral heroes; rather they are gifts of God to all the baptized: in them our life develops, too. The beginning is also the end, the starting point is also the point of arrival: the whole journey toward an ever more radical realization of faith, hope, and charity. The whole ascent is present in these virtues. Faith is fundamental, because this virtue implies that I renounce my arrogance, my thought, and the claim to judge by myself without entrusting myself to others. This journey toward humility, toward spiritual childhood is essential. It is necessary to overcome the attitude of arrogance that makes one say: I know better, in this my time of the twenty-first century, than what people could have known then. Instead, it is necessary to entrust oneself to Sacred Scripture alone, to the Word of the Lord, to look out on the horizon of faith with humility, in order to enter into the enormous immensity of the universal world, of the world of God. In this way our soul grows, the sensitivity of the heart grows toward God. Rightly, John Climacus says that hope alone renders us capable of living charity; hope in which we transcend the things of every day; we do not expect success in our earthly days, but we look forward to the revelation of God himself at last. It is only in this extension of our soul, in this self-transcendence, that our life becomes great and that we are able to bear the effort and disappointments of every day, that we can be kind to others without expecting any reward. Only if there is God, this great hope to which I aspire, can I take the small steps of my life and thus learn charity. The mystery of prayer, of the personal knowledge of Jesus, is concealed in charity: simple prayer that strives only to move the divine Teacher's heart. So it is that one's own heart opens, one learns from him his own kindness, his love. Let us therefore use this "ascent" of faith, hope, and charity. In this way we will arrive at true life.

Saint Bede, the Venerable

WEDNESDAY, 18 FEBRUARY 2009
Saint Peter's Square

Dear Brothers and Sisters,

The Saint we are approaching today is called Bede and was born in the northeast of England, to be exact, Northumbria, in the year 672 or 673. He himself recounts that when he was seven years old his parents entrusted him to the Abbot of the neighboring Benedictine monastery to be educated: "spending all the remaining time of my life a dweller in that monastery". He recalls, "I wholly applied myself to the study of Scripture; and amidst the observance of the monastic *Rule* and the daily charge of singing in church, I always took delight in learning, or teaching, or writing" (*Historia eccl. Anglorum*, V, 24). In fact, Bede became one of the most outstanding erudite figures of the early Middle Ages since he was able to avail himself of many precious manuscripts which his Abbots would bring him on their return from frequent journeys to the Continent and to Rome. His teaching and the fame of his writings occasioned his friendships with many of the most important figures of his time, who encouraged him to persevere in his work from which so many were to benefit. When Bede fell ill, he did not stop working, always preserving an inner joy that he expressed in prayer and song. He ended his most important work, the *Historia Ecclesiastica gentis Anglorum*, with this invocation: "I beseech you, O good Jesus, that to the one to whom you have graciously granted sweetly to drink in the words of your knowledge, you will also vouchsafe in your loving kindness that he may one day come to you, the Fountain of all wisdom, and appear for ever before your face". Death took him on 26 May 737: it was the Ascension.

Sacred Scripture was the constant source of Bede's theological reflection. After a critical study of the text (a copy of the monumental *Codex Amiatinus* of the Vulgate on which Bede worked has come down to us), he comments on the Bible, interpreting it in a Christological key, that is, combining two things: on the one hand, he listens to exactly what the text says, he really seeks to hear and understand the text itself; on the other, he is convinced that the key to understanding Sacred Scripture as the one Word of God is Christ, and with Christ, in his light, one understands the Old and New Testaments as "one" Sacred Scripture. The events of the Old and New Testaments go together; they are the way to Christ, although expressed in different signs and institutions (this is what he calls the *concordia sacramentorum*). For example, the tent of the covenant that Moses pitched in the desert and the first and second temple of Jerusalem are images of the Church, the new temple built on Christ and on the Apostles with living stones, held together by the love of the Spirit. And just as pagan peoples also contributed to building the ancient temple by making available valuable materials and the technical experience of their master builders, so too contributing to the construction of the Church there were apostles and teachers, not only from ancient Jewish, Greek, and Latin lineage, but also from the new peoples, among whom Bede was pleased to list the Irish Celts and Anglo-Saxons. Saint Bede saw the growth of the universal dimension of the Church, which is not restricted to one specific culture but is comprised of all the cultures of the world that must be open to Christ and find in him their goal.

Another of Bede's favorite topics is the history of the Church. After studying the period described in the Acts of the Apostles, he reviews the history of the Fathers and the Councils, convinced that the work of the Holy Spirit continues in history. In the *Chronica Maiora*, Bede outlines a chronology that was to become the basis of the universal Calendar *"ab incarnatione Domini"*. In his day, time was calculated from the foundation of the City of Rome. Realizing that the true reference point, the center of history, is the Birth of Christ, Bede gave us this calendar that interprets history starting from the Incarnation of the Lord. Bede records the first six Ecumenical Councils and their developments faithfully presenting Christian doctrine, both Mariological and soteriological, and denouncing the Monophysite and Monothelite, Iconoclastic and Neo-Pelagian heresies. Lastly he compiled with documentary rigor and literary expertise the *Ecclesiastical History of the English Peoples* mentioned above, which earned him recognition as "the father of English historiography". The characteristic features of the Church that Bede sought to emphasize are: a) *catholicity*, seen as faithfulness to tradition while remaining open to historical developments and as the quest for unity in multiplicity, in historical and cultural diversity according to the directives Pope Gregory the Great had given to Augustine of Canterbury, the Apostle of England; b) *apostolicity and Roman traditions:* in this regard he deemed it of prime importance to convince all the Irish, Celtic, and Pict Churches to have one celebration for Easter in accordance with the

Roman calendar. The *computus* which he worked out scientifically to establish the exact date of the Easter celebration, hence the entire cycle of the liturgical year, became the reference text for the whole Catholic Church.

Bede was also an eminent teacher of liturgical theology. In his homilies on the Gospels for Sundays and feast days, he achieves a true mystagogy, teaching the faithful to celebrate the mysteries of the faith joyfully and to reproduce them coherently in life, while awaiting their full manifestation with the return of Christ, when, with our glorified bodies, we shall be admitted to the offertory procession in the eternal liturgy of God in Heaven. Following the "realism" of the catecheses of Cyril, Ambrose, and Augustine, Bede teaches that the sacraments of Christian initiation make every faithful person "not only a Christian but Christ". Indeed, every time that a faithful soul lovingly accepts and preserves the Word of God, in imitation of Mary, he conceives and generates Christ anew. And every time that a group of neophytes receives the Easter sacraments, the Church "reproduces herself" or, to use a more daring term, the Church becomes "Mother of God", participating in the generation of her children through the action of the Holy Spirit.

By his way of creating theology, interweaving the Bible, liturgy, and history, Bede has a timely message for the different "states of life": a) for scholars (*doctores ac doctrices*) he recalls two essential tasks: to examine the marvels of the Word of God in order to present them in an attractive form to the faithful; to explain the dogmatic truths, avoiding heretical complications and keeping to "Catholic simplicity", with the attitude of the lowly and humble to whom God is pleased to reveal the mysteries of the Kingdom; b) pastors, for their part, must give priority to preaching, not only through verbal or hagiographic language, but also by giving importance to icons, processions, and pilgrimages. Bede recommends that they use the vernacular as he himself does, explaining the "Our Father" and the "Creed" in Northumbrian and continuing, until the last day of his life, his commentary on the Gospel of John in the vernacular; c) Bede recommends to consecrated people who devote themselves to the Divine Office, living in the joy of fraternal communion and progressing in the spiritual life by means of ascesis and contemplation, that they attend to the apostolate—no one possesses the Gospel for himself alone but must perceive it as a gift for others, too—both by collaborating with Bishops in pastoral activities of various kinds for the young Christian communities and by offering themselves for the evangelizing mission among the pagans, outside their own country, as "*peregrini pro amore Dei*".

Making this viewpoint his own, in his commentary on the Song of Songs, Bede presents the Synagogue and the Church as collaborators in the dissemination of God's Word. Christ the Bridegroom wants a hard-working Church, "weathered by the efforts of evangelization"—there is a clear reference to the word in the Song of Songs (1:5), where the bride says "*Nigra sum sed formosa*" ("I am very dark, but comely")—intent on tilling other fields or vineyards and in establishing among the new peoples "not a temporary hut but a permanent dwelling place", in other words, intent on integrating the Gospel into their social fabric and cultural institutions. In this perspective the holy Doctor urges lay faithful to be diligent in religious instruction, imitating those "insatiable crowds of the Gospel who did not even allow the Apostles time to take a mouthful". He teaches them how to pray ceaselessly, "reproducing in life what they celebrate in the liturgy", offering all their actions as a spiritual sacrifice in union with Christ. He explains to parents that in their small domestic circle, too, they can exercise "the priestly office as pastors and guides", giving their children a Christian upbringing. He also affirms that he knows many of the faithful (men and women, married and single) "capable of irreproachable conduct who, if appropriately guided, will be able every day to receive Eucharistic communion" (*Epist. ad Ecgberctum*, ed. Plummer, p. 419).

The fame of holiness and wisdom that Bede already enjoyed in his lifetime earned him the title of "Venerable". Pope Sergius I called him this when he wrote to his Abbot in 701 asking him to allow him to come to Rome temporarily to give advice on matters of universal interest. After his death, Bede's writings were widely disseminated in his homeland and on the European Continent. Bishop Saint Boniface, the great missionary of Germany (d. 754), asked the Archbishop of York and the Abbot of Wearmouth several times to have some of his works transcribed and sent to him so that he and his companions might also enjoy the spiritual light that shone from them. A century later, Notker Balbulus, Abbot of Sankt Gallen (d. 912), noting the extraordinary influence of Bede, compared him to a new sun that God had caused to rise, not in the East but in the West, to illuminate the world. Apart from the rhetorical emphasis, it is a fact that with his works Bede made an effective contribution to building a Christian Europe in which the various peoples and cultures amalgamated with one another, thereby giving them a single physiognomy, inspired by the Christian faith. Let us pray that today, too, there may be figures of Bede's stature to keep the whole Continent united; let us pray that we may all be willing to rediscover our common roots in order to be builders of a profoundly human and authentically Christian Europe.

13

Saint Boniface, the Apostle
of the Germans

WEDNESDAY, 11 MARCH 2009
Saint Peter's Square

Dear Brothers and Sisters,

Today, we shall reflect on a great eighth-century missionary who spread Christianity in Central Europe, indeed also in my own country: Saint Boniface, who has gone down in history as "the Apostle of the Germans". We have a fair amount of information on his life, thanks to the diligence of his biographers. He was born into an Anglo-Saxon family in Wessex in about 675 and was baptized with the name of Winfrid. He entered the monastery at a very early age, attracted by the monastic ideal. Since he possessed considerable intellectual ability, he seemed destined for a peaceful and brilliant academic career. He became a teacher of Latin grammar, wrote several treatises, and even composed various poems in Latin. He was ordained a priest at the age of about thirty and felt called to an apostolate among the pagans on the Continent. His country, Great Britain, which had been evangelized barely one hundred years earlier by Benedictines led by Saint Augustine, at the time showed such sound faith and ardent charity that it could send missionaries to Central Europe to proclaim the Gospel there. In 716, Winfrid went to Frisia (today Holland) with a few companions, but he encountered the opposition of the local chieftain, and his attempt at evangelization failed. Having returned home, he did not lose heart and two years later traveled to Rome to speak to Pope Gregory II and receive his instructions. One biographer recounts that the Pope welcomed him "with a smile and a look full of kindliness" and had "important conversations" with him in the following days (Willibald, *Vita S. Bonifatii*, ed. Levison, pp. 13–14) and lastly, after conferring upon him the new name of Boniface, assigned to him, in official letters, the mission of preaching the Gospel among the German peoples.

Comforted and sustained by the Pope's support, Boniface embarked on the preaching of the Gospel in those regions, fighting against pagan worship and reinforcing the foundations of human and Christian morality. With a deep sense of duty he wrote in one of his letters: "We are united in the fight on the Lord's Day, because days of affliction and wretchedness have come.... We are not mute dogs or taciturn observers or mercenaries fleeing from wolves! On the contrary, we are diligent pastors who watch over Christ's flock, who proclaim God's will to the leaders and ordinary folk, to the rich and the poor ... in season and out of season ..." (cf. *Epistulae*, 3,352.354: MGH). With his tireless activity, his gift for organization, and his adaptable, friendly, yet firm, character, Boniface obtained great results. The Pope then "declared that he wished to confer upon him the episcopal dignity so that he might thus with greater determination correct and lead back to the path of truth those who had strayed, feeling supported by the greater authority of the apostolic dignity and being much more readily accepted by all in the office of preacher, the clearer it was that this was why he had been ordained by the Apostolic Bishop" (Othlo, *Vita S. Bonifatii*, ed. Levison, lib. I, p. 127).

The Supreme Pontiff himself consecrated Boniface "Regional Bishop", that is, for the whole of Germany. Boniface then resumed his apostolic labors in the territories assigned to him and extended his action also to the Church of the Gauls: with great caution he restored discipline in the Church, convoked various Synods to guarantee the authority of the sacred canons, and strengthened the necessary communion with the Roman Pontiff, a point that he had very much at heart. The Successors of Pope Gregory II also held him in the highest esteem. Gregory III appointed him Archbishop of all the Germanic tribes, sent him the pallium, and granted him the faculties to organize the ecclesiastical hierarchy in those regions (cf. *Epist* 28; *S. Bonifatii Epistulae*, ed. Tangl, Berolini, 1916). Pope Zacchary confirmed him in his office and praised his dedication (cf. *Epist.* 51, 57, 58, 60, 68, 77, 80, 86, 87, 89: *op. cit.*); Pope Stephen III, newly elected, received a letter from him in which he expressed his filial respect (cf. *Epist.* 108: *op. cit.*).

In addition to this work of evangelization and organization of the Church through the founding of dioceses and the celebration of Synods, this great Bishop did not omit to encourage the foundation of various male and female monasteries so that they would become like beacons, so as to radiate human and Christian culture and the faith in the territory. He summoned monks and nuns from the Benedictine monastic communities in his homeland who gave him a most effective and invaluable help in proclaiming the Gospel and in disseminating the humanities and the arts among the population. Indeed, he rightly considered that work for the Gospel must also be work for a true human

culture. Above all the Monastery of Fulda—founded in about
743—was the heart and center of outreach of religious spirituality and culture: there the monks, in prayer, work, and
penance, strove to achieve holiness; there they trained in
the study of the sacred and profane disciplines and prepared
themselves for the proclamation of the Gospel in order to
be missionaries. Thus it was to the credit of Boniface, of
his monks and nuns—for women, too, had a very important role in this work of evangelization—that human culture, which is inseparable from faith and reveals its beauty,
flourished. Boniface himself has left us an important intellectual corpus. First of all is his copious correspondence, in
which pastoral letters alternate with official letters and others private in nature, which record social events but above
all reveal his richly human temperament and profound faith.
In addition, he composed a treatise on the *Ars grammatica*
in which he explained the declensions, verbs, and syntax of
the Latin language, but which also became for him a means
of spreading culture and the faith. An *Ars metrica*, that is, an
introduction on how to write poetry, as well as various poetic
compositions and, lastly, a collection of fifteen sermons are
also attributed to him.

Although he was getting on in years (he was almost eighty),
he prepared himself for a new evangelizing mission: with
about fifty monks he returned to Frisia, where he had begun
his work. Almost as a prediction of his imminent death, in
alluding to the journey of life, he wrote to Bishop Lull, his
disciple and successor in the See of Mainz: "I wish to bring
to a conclusion the purpose of this journey; in no way can
I renounce my desire to set out. The day of my end is near,
and the time of my death is approaching; having shed my
mortal body, I shall rise to the eternal reward. May you,
my dear son, ceaselessly call the people from the maze of

error, complete the building of the Basilica of Fulda that has already been begun, and in it lay my body, worn out by the long years of life" (Willibald, *Vita S. Bonifatii, ed. cit.*, p. 46). While he was beginning the celebration of Mass at Dokkum (in what today is northern Holland) on 5 June 754, he was assaulted by a band of pagans. Advancing with a serene expression, he "forbade his followers from fighting, saying, 'cease, my sons, from fighting, give up warfare, for the witness of Scripture recommends that we do not give an eye for an eye but rather good for evil. Here is the long-awaited day; the time of our end has now come; courage in the Lord!'" (*ibid.*, pp. 49–50). These were his last words before he fell under the blows of his aggressors. The mortal remains of the Martyr Bishop were then taken to the Monastery of Fulda, where they received a fitting burial. One of his first biographers had already made this judgment of him: "The holy Bishop Boniface can call himself father of all the inhabitants of Germany, for it was he who first brought them forth in Christ with the words of his holy preaching; he strengthened them with his example; and lastly, he gave his life for them; no greater love than this can be shown" (Othlo, *Vita S. Bonifatii, ed. cit.*, lib. I, p. 158).

Centuries later, what message can we gather today from the teaching and marvelous activity of this great missionary and martyr? For those who approach Boniface, an initial fact stands out: *the centrality of the Word of God*, lived and interpreted in the faith of the Church, a Word that he lived, preached, and witnessed to until he gave the supreme gift of himself in martyrdom. He was so passionate about the Word of God that he felt the urgent need and duty to communicate it to others, even at his own personal risk. This Word was the pillar of the faith which he had committed himself to spreading at the moment of his episcopal ordination: "I profess integrally the purity of the holy Catholic faith, and with the help of God I desire to remain in the unity of this faith, in which there is no doubt that the salvation of Christians lies" (*Epist.* 12, in *S. Bonifatii Epistolae, ed. cit.*, p. 29). The second most important proof that emerges from the life of Boniface is his *faithful communion with the Apostolic See*, which was a firm and central reference point of his missionary work; he always preserved this communion as a rule of his mission and left it, as it were, as his will. In a letter to Pope Zachary, he said: "I never cease to invite and to submit to obedience to the Apostolic See those who desire to remain in the Catholic faith and in the unity of the Roman Church and all those whom God grants to me as listeners and disciples in my mission" (*Epist.* 50: in *ibid.*, p. 81). One result of this commitment was the steadfast spirit of cohesion around the Successor of Peter which Boniface transmitted to the Church in his mission territory, uniting England, Germany, and France with Rome and thereby effectively contributing to planting those Christian roots of Europe which were to produce abundant fruit in the centuries to come. Boniface also deserves our attention for a third characteristic: he encouraged *the encounter between the Christian-Roman culture and the Germanic culture*. Indeed, he knew that humanizing and evangelizing culture was an integral part of his mission as Bishop. In passing on the ancient patrimony of Christian values, he grafted on to the Germanic populations a new, more human life-style, thanks to which the inalienable rights of the person were more widely respected. As a true son of Saint Benedict, he was able to combine prayer and labor (manual and intellectual), pen and plough.

Boniface's courageous witness is an invitation to us all to welcome God's Word into our lives as an essential reference point, to love the Church passionately, to feel jointly responsible for her future, to seek her unity around the Successor of Peter. At the same time, he reminds us that Christianity, by encouraging the dissemination of culture, furthers human progress. It is now up to us to be equal to such a prestigious patrimony and to make it fructify for the benefit of the generations to come.

His ardent zeal for the Gospel never fails to impress me. At the age of forty-one, he left a beautiful and fruitful monastic life, the life of a monk and teacher, in order to proclaim the Gospel to the simple, to barbarians; once again, at the age of eighty, he went to a region in which he foresaw his martyrdom. By comparing his ardent faith, this zeal for the Gospel, with our own often lukewarm and bureaucratized faith, we see what we must do and how to renew our faith, in order to give the precious pearl of the Gospel as a gift to our time.

14

Ambrose Autpert

Dear Brothers and Sisters,

The Church lives in people, and those who want to know the Church better, to understand her mystery, must consider the people who have seen and lived her message, her mystery. In the Wednesday Catechesis I have therefore been speaking for some time of people from whom we can learn what the Church is. We began with the Apostles and Fathers of the Church, and we have gradually reached the eighth century, Charlemagne's period. Today I want to talk about Ambrose Autpert, a lesser known author; in fact, the majority of his works were attributed to other, better known people, from Saint Ambrose of Milan to Saint Ildefonsus, not to mention those that the monks of Monte Cassino claimed to have come from the pen of an Abbot of theirs of the same name who lived almost a century later. Apart from a few brief autobiographical notes in his important commentary on the *Apocalypse*, we have little information about his life. Yet, an attentive reading of the works whose authorship criticism has gradually attributed to him makes it possible to discover in his teaching a precious theological and spiritual treasure for our time, too.

Born into a noble family in Provence—according to his future biographer, Giovanni—Ambrose Autpert was at the court of the Frankish King Pepin the Short, where, in addition to his function as official, he somehow also played the role of tutor to the future Emperor Charlemagne. Autpert, probably in the retinue of Pope Stephen II, who in 753–54 went to the Frankish court, came to Italy and had the opportunity of visiting the famous Benedictine Abbey of Saint Vincent, located near the sources of the River Volturno in the Duchy of Benevento. Founded at the beginning of the century by three brothers from Benevento—Paldone, Tatone, and Tasone—the abbey was known as an oasis of classical and Christian culture. Shortly after his visit, Ambrose Autpert decided to embrace the religious life and entered that monastery, where he acquired an appropriate education, especially in the fields of theology and spirituality, in accordance with the tradition of the Fathers. In about the year 761, he was ordained a priest, and on 4 October 777 he was elected Abbot with the support of the Frankish monks despite the opposition of the Lombards, who favored Potone the Lombard. The nationalistic tension in the background did not diminish in the subsequent months. As a result, in the following year, 778, Autpert decided to resign and to seek shelter, together with several Frankish monks, in Spoleto, where he could count on Charlemagne's protection. This, however, did not solve the dissension at Saint Vincent's Monastery. A few years later, when on the death of the Abbot who had succeeded Autpert, Potone himself was elected as his successor (782), the dispute flared up again and even led to the denunciation of the new Abbot to Charlemagne. The latter sent the contenders to the tribunal of the Pontiff, who summoned them to Rome. Autpert was also called as a witness. However, he died suddenly on the journey, perhaps murdered, on 30 January 784.

Ambrose Autpert was a monk and Abbot in an epoch marked by strong political tensions which also had repercussions on life within the monasteries. We have frequent and disturbing echoes of them in his writings. He reports, for example, the contradiction between the splendid external appearance of monasteries and the tepidity of the monks: this criticism was also certainly directed at his own abbey. He wrote for his monastery the *Life* of the three founders with the clear intention of offering the new generation of monks a term of reference by which to measure themselves. He also pursued a similar aim in a small ascetic treatise, *Conflictus vitiorum atque virtutum* ("Combat between the vices and the virtues"), which met with great acclaim in the Middle Ages and was published in 1473 in Utrecht, under Gregory the Great's name, and, a year later, in Strasbourg under that of Saint Augustine. In it Ambrose Autpert intends to give the monks a practical training in how to face spiritual combat day after day. Significantly, he applies the affirmation in 2 Timothy 3:12: "All who desire to live a godly life in Christ Jesus will be persecuted", no longer by external forces, but by the assault that the Christian must face within himself on the part of the forces of evil. Twenty-four pairs of fighters are presented in a sort of disputation: every vice seeks to lure the soul by subtle reasoning, whereas the respective virtue refutes these claims, preferably by using words of Scripture.

In this treatise on the combat between the vices and the virtues, Autpert sets *contemptus mundi* (contempt for the world) against *cupiditas* (greed), which becomes an important figure in the spirituality of monks. This contempt for the world is not a contempt for Creation, for the beauty

and goodness of Creation and of the Creator, but a contempt for the false vision of the world that is presented to
us and suggested to us precisely by covetousness. It insin-
uates that "having" is the supreme value of our being, of
our life in the world, and seems important. And thus it
falsifies the creation of the world and destroys the world.
Autpert then remarks that the acquisitive greed of the rich
and powerful in the society of his time also exists within
the souls of monks, and thus he writes a treatise entitled *De
cupiditate*, in which, together with the Apostle Paul, he
denounces greed from the outset as the root of all evil. He
writes: "In the earth's soil various sharp thorns spring from
different roots; in the human heart, on the other hand, the
stings of all the vices sprout from a single root, greed" (*De
cupiditate* 1: CCCM 27B, p. 963). In the light of the present
global financial crisis, the full timeliness of this observation
is revealed. We see that it was precisely from this root of
covetousness that the crisis sprang. Ambrose imagines the
objection that the rich and powerful might raise, saying:
but we are not monks; certain ascetic requirements do not
apply to us. And he answers: "What you say is true, but for
you, in the manner of your class and in accordance with
your strength, the straight and narrow way applies because
the Lord has proposed only two doors and two ways (that
is, the narrow door and the wide door, the steep road and
the easy one); he has not pointed to a third door or a third
way" (*loc. cit.*, p. 978). He sees clearly that life-styles differ
widely. Nonetheless, the duty to combat greed, to fight the
desire to possess, to appear, and the false concept of freedom as the faculty to dispose of all things as one pleases
applies to the man in this world, too, and also to the rich.
The rich person must also find the authentic road of truth,
of love, and thus of an upright life. As a prudent pastor of

souls, Autpert was then able to speak a word of comfort at the end of his penitential homily: "I have not spoken against the greedy, but against greed, not against nature, but against vice" (*loc. cit.*, p. 981).

Ambrose Autpert's most important work is without a doubt his commentary on the *Apocalypse* [*Expositio in Apocalypsim*] in ten volumes: this constitutes, centuries later, the first comprehensive commentary in the Latin world on the last book of Sacred Scripture. This work was the fruit of many years' work, carried out in two phases between 758 and 767, hence prior to his election as Abbot. In the premise he is careful to indicate his sources, something that was not usual in the Middle Ages. Through what was perhaps his most significant source, the commentary of Bishop Primasius of Hadrumetum, written in about the middle of the sixth century, Autpert came into contact with the interpretation of the *Apocalypse* bequeathed to us by Ticonius, an African who lived a generation before Saint Augustine. He was not a Catholic; he belonged to the schismatic Donatist Church, yet he was a great theologian. In his commentary he sees the *Apocalypse* above all as a reflection of the mystery of the Church. Ticonius had reached the conviction that the Church was a bipartite body: on the one hand, he says, she belongs to Christ, but there is another part of the Church that belongs to the devil. Augustine read this commentary and profited from it but strongly emphasized that the Church is in Christ's hands, that she remains his Body, forming one subject with him, sharing in the mediation of grace. He therefore stresses that the Church can never be separated from Jesus Christ. In his interpretation of the *Apocalypse*, similar to that of Ticonius, Autpert is not so much concerned with the Second Coming of Christ at the end of time as rather with the consequences that derive for the Church of the present from his

First Coming, his Incarnation in the womb of the Virgin Mary. And he speaks very important words to us: in reality Christ "must be born, die, and be raised daily in us, who are his Body" (*In Apoc.*, III: CCCM, 27, p. 205). In the context of the mystic dimension that invests every Christian, he looks to Mary as a model of the Church, a model for all of us, because Christ must also be born in and among us. Under the guidance of the Fathers, who saw the "woman clothed with the sun" of Revelation 12:1 as an image of the Church, Autpert argues: "the Blessed and devout Virgin ... daily gives birth to new peoples from which the general Body of the Mediator is formed. It is therefore not surprising if she, in whose blessed womb the Church herself deserved to be united with her Head, represents the type of the Church." In this sense Autpert considers the Virgin Mary's role decisive in the work of the redemption (cf. also his homilies *In purificatione S. Mariae* and *In adsumptione S. Mariae*). His great veneration and profound love for the Mother of God sometimes inspired in him formulations that in a certain way anticipated those of Saint Bernard and of Franciscan mysticism, yet without ever deviating to disputable forms of sentimentalism because he never separates Mary from the mystery of the Church. Therefore, with good reason, Ambrose Autpert is considered the first great Mariologist in the West. He considers that the profound study of the sacred sciences, especially meditation on the Sacred Scriptures, which he describes as "the ineffable sky, the unfathomable abyss", should be combined with the devotion that he believed must free the soul from attachment to earthly and transient pleasures (*In Apoc.* IX). In the beautiful prayer with which his commentary on the *Apocalypse* ends, underlining the priority that must be given to love in all theological research, he addresses God with these words: "When you are intellectually examined by us, you are not revealed as you truly are: when you are loved, you are attained."

Today we can see in Ambrose Autpert a personality who lived in a time of powerful political exploitation of the Church, in which nationalism and tribalism had disfigured the face of the Church. But he, in the midst of all these difficulties with which we too are familiar, was able to discover the true face of the Church in Mary, in the Saints, and he was thus able to understand what it means to be a Catholic, to be a Christian, to live on the Word of God, to enter into this abyss, and thus to live the mystery of the Mother of God: to give new life to the Word of God, to offer to the Word of God one's own flesh in the present time. And with all his theological knowledge, the depth of his knowledge, Autpert was able to understand that with merely theological research God cannot truly be known as he is. Love alone reaches him. Let us hear this message and pray the Lord to help us to live the mystery of the Church today in our time.

15

Germanus of Constantinople

WEDNESDAY, 29 APRIL 2009
Saint Peter's Square

Dear Brothers and Sisters,

Patriarch Germanus of Constantinople, about whom I would like to talk today, does not belong among the most representative figures of the Greek-speaking world of Eastern Christianity. Yet, his name appears with a certain solemnity in the list of the great champions of sacred images drafted by the Second Council of Nicaea, the seventh Ecumenical Council (787). The Greek Church celebrates his Feast in the liturgy of 12 May. He played an important role in the complex history of the controversy over images during the "Iconoclastic Crisis": he was able to resist effectively the pressures of an Iconoclast Emperor, in other words, one opposed to icons, such as Leo III.

During the patriarchate of Germanus (715–730), the capital of the Byzantine Empire, Constantinople, was subjected to a dangerous siege by the Saracens. On that occasion (717–718), a solemn procession was organized in the city displaying the image of the Mother of God, the *Theotokos*, and the relic of the True Cross, to invoke protection for the city from on high. In fact, Constantinople was liberated from the siege. The enemy decided to desist for ever from the idea of establishing their capital in the city that was the symbol of the Christian Empire, and the people were extremely grateful for the divine help.

After that event, Patriarch Germanus was convinced that God's intervention must be considered as obvious approval of the devotion shown by the people for the holy icons. However, Emperor Leo III was of the absolute opposite opinion; that very year (717) he was enthroned as the undisputed Emperor in the capital, over which he reigned until 741. After the liberation of Constantinople and after a series of other victories, the Christian Emperor began to show more and more openly his conviction that the consolidation of the Empire must begin precisely with a reordering of the manifestations of faith, with particular reference to the risk of idolatry to which, in his opinion, the people were prone because of their excessive worship of icons.

Patriarch Germanus' appeal to the tradition of the Church and to the actual efficacy of certain images unanimously recognized as "miraculous" were to no avail. The Emperor more and more stubbornly applied his restoration project, which provided for the elimination of icons. At a public meeting on 7 January 730, when he openly took a stance against the worship of images, Germanus was in no way ready to comply with the Emperor's will on matters he himself deemed crucial for the Orthodox faith, of which he believed veneration and love for images were part. As a consequence, Germanus was forced to resign from the office of Patriarch, condemning himself to exile in a monastery where he died forgotten by almost all. His name reappeared on the occasion of the Second Council of Nicaea (787), when the Orthodox Fathers decided in favor of icons, recognizing the merits of Germanus.

Patriarch Germanus took great care of the liturgical celebrations and, for a certain time, was also believed to have
introduced the feast of the *Akathistos*. As is well known, the
Akathistos is a famous ancient hymn to the *Theotokos*, the
Mother of God, that came into being in the Byzantine context. Despite the fact that from the theological viewpoint Germanus cannot be described as a great thinker, some of his
works had a certain resonance, especially on account of some
of his insights concerning *Mariology*. In fact, various of his
homilies on Marian topics are extant, and some of them profoundly marked the piety of entire generations of faithful,
both in the East and in the West. His splendid *Homilies on the
Presentation of Mary at the Temple* are still living testimony of
the unwritten tradition of the Christian Churches. Generations of nuns and monks and the members of a great number
of institutes of consecrated life continue still today to find in
these texts the most precious pearls of spirituality.

Some of Germanus' Mariological texts still give rise to
wonder today. They are part of the homilies he gave *In SS.
Deiparae dormitionem*, a celebration that corresponds with our
Feast of the Assumption. Among these texts Pope Pius XII
picked out one that he set like a pearl in his Apostolic Constitution *Munificentissimus Deus* (1950), with which he declared
Mary's Assumption a Dogma of faith. Pope Pius XII cited
this text in the above-mentioned Constitution, presenting
it as one of the arguments in favor of the permanent faith
of the Church concerning the bodily Assumption of Mary
into Heaven. Germanus wrote:

> Could it ever happen, Most Holy Mother of God, that
> Heaven and earth feel honored by your presence, and you,
> with your departure, leave men and women without your
> protection? No. It is impossible to think such things. In

fact, just as when you were in the world you did not feel foreign to the realities of Heaven, so too after you had emigrated from this world, you were not foreign to the possibility of communicating in spirit with mankind.... You did not at all abandon those to whom you had guaranteed salvation ... in fact, your spirit lives in eternity, nor did your flesh suffer the corruption of the tomb. You, O Mother, are close to all and protect all, and although our eyes are unable to see you, we know, O Most Holy One, that you dwell among all of us and make yourself present in the most varied ways.... You (Mary), reveal your whole self, as is written, in your beauty. Your virginal body is entirely holy, entirely chaste, entirely the dwelling place of God so that, even for this reason, it is absolutely incorruptible. It is unchangeable since what was human in it has been taken up in incorruptibility, remaining alive and absolutely glorious, undamaged, and sharing in perfect life. Indeed, it was impossible that the one who had become the vase of God and the living temple of the most holy divinity of the Only Begotten One be enclosed in the sepulcher of the dead. On the other hand, we believe with certainty that you continue to walk with us. (*PG* 98, 344B–346B, passim)

It has been said that for the Byzantines the decorum of the rhetorical form in preaching and especially in hymns or in the poetic compositions that they call *troparia* is equally important in the liturgical celebration as the beauty of the sacred building in which it takes place. Patriarch Germanus was recognized, in that tradition, as one who made a great contribution to keeping this conviction alive, that is, that the beauty of the words and language must coincide with the beauty of the building and the music.

I quote, to conclude, the inspired words with which Germanus described the Church at the beginning of his small masterpiece:

The Church is the temple of God, a sacred space, a house of prayer, the convocation of people, the Body of Christ. . . . She is Heaven on earth where the transcendent God dwells as if in his own home and passes through, but she is also an impression made (*antitypos*) of the Crucifixion, the tomb, and the Resurrection. . . . The Church is God's house in which the life-giving mystical sacrifice is celebrated, at the same time the most intimate part of the shrine and sacred grotto. Within her, in fact, the sepulcher and the table are found, nourishment for the soul and a guarantee of life. In her, lastly, are found those true and proper precious pearls which are the divine dogmas of teaching that the Lord offered directly to his disciples. (*PG* 98, 384B–385A)

Lastly, the question remains: what does this Saint chronologically and also culturally rather distant from us have to tell us today? I am thinking mainly of three things. The first: there is a certain visibility of God in the world, in the Church, that we must learn to perceive. God has created man in his image, but this image was covered with the scum of so much sin that God almost no longer shines through it. Thus the Son of God was made true man, a perfect image of God: thus in Christ we may also contemplate the Face of God and learn to be true men ourselves, true images of God. Christ invites us to imitate him, to become similar to him, so in every person the Face of God shines out anew. To tell the truth, in the Ten Commandments God forbade the making of images of God, but this was because of the temptations to idolatry to which the believer might be exposed in a context of paganism. Yet when God made himself visible in Christ through the Incarnation, it became legitimate to reproduce the Face of Christ. The holy images teach us to see God represented in the Face of Christ. After the Incarnation of the Son of God, it therefore became possible to see God in images of Christ and also in the faces of the Saints, in the faces of all people in whom God's holiness shines out.

The second thing is the beauty and dignity of the liturgy. To celebrate the liturgy in the awareness of God's presence, with that dignity and beauty which make a little of his splendor visible, is the commitment of every Christian trained in his faith. The third thing is to love the Church. Precisely with regard to the Church, we men and women are prompted to see above all the sins and the negative side, but with the help of faith, which enables us to see in an authentic way, today and always we can rediscover the divine beauty in her. It is in the Church that God is present, offers himself to us in the Holy Eucharist, and remains present for adoration. In the Church God speaks to us; in the Church God "walks beside us", as Saint Germanus said. In the Church we receive God's forgiveness and learn to forgive.

Let us pray God to teach us to see his presence and his beauty in the Church, to see his presence in the world, and to help us, too, to be transparent to his light.

16

John Damascene

Dear Brothers and Sisters,

Today I should like to speak about John Damascene, a personage of prime importance in the history of Byzantine theology, a great Doctor in the history of the Universal Church. Above all, he was an eyewitness of the passage from the Greek and Syrian Christian cultures shared by the Eastern part of the Byzantine Empire to the Islamic culture, which spread through its military conquests in the territory commonly known as the Middle or Near East. John, born into a wealthy Christian family, at an early age assumed the role, perhaps already held by his father, of Treasurer of the Caliphate. Very soon, however, dissatisfied with life at court, he decided on a monastic life and entered the monastery of Mar Saba, near Jerusalem. This was around the year 700. He never again left the monastery but dedicated all his energy to ascesis and literary work, not disdaining a certain amount of pastoral activity, as is shown by his numerous homilies. His liturgical commemoration is on 4 December. Pope Leo XIII proclaimed him Doctor of the Universal Church in 1890.

In the East, his best remembered works are the three *Discourses against those who calumniate the Holy Images*, which were condemned after his death by the Iconoclastic Council of Hieria (754). These discourses, however, were also the fundamental grounds for his rehabilitation and canonization on the part of the Orthodox Fathers summoned to the Council of Nicaea (787), the Seventh Ecumenical Council. In these texts it is possible to trace the first important theological attempts to legitimize the veneration of sacred images, relating them to the mystery of the Incarnation of the Son of God in the womb of the Virgin Mary.

John Damascene was also among the first to distinguish, in the cult, both public and private, of the Christians, between worship (*latreia*) and veneration (*proskynesis*): the first can only be offered to God, spiritual above all else; the second, on the other hand, can make use of an image to address the one whom the image represents. Obviously the Saint can in no way be identified with the material of which the icon is composed. This distinction was immediately seen to be very important in finding an answer in Christian terms to those who considered universal and eternal the strict Old Testament prohibition against the use of cult images. This was also a matter of great debate in the Islamic world, which accepts the Jewish tradition of the total exclusion of cult images. Christians, on the other hand, in this context, have discussed the problem and found a justification for the veneration of images. John Damascene writes,

> In other ages God had not been represented in images, being incorporate and faceless. But since God has now been seen in the flesh and lived among men, I represent that part of God which is visible. I do not venerate matter, but the Creator of matter, who became matter for my sake and deigned to live in matter and bring about my salvation through matter. I will not cease therefore to venerate that matter through which my salvation was achieved. But

I do not venerate it in absolute terms as God! How could
that which, from non-existence, has been given existence
be God? ... But I also venerate and respect all the rest of
matter which has brought me salvation, since it is full of
energy and holy graces. Is not the wood of the Cross,
three times blessed, matter? ... And the ink, and the most
Holy Book of the Gospels, are they not matter? The
redeeming altar which dispenses the Bread of life, is it not
matter? ... And, before all else, are not the flesh and blood
of Our Lord matter? Either we must suppress the sacred
nature of all these things, or we must concede to the tradition of the Church the veneration of the images of God
and that of the friends of God who are sanctified by the
name they bear and, for this reason, are possessed by the
grace of the Holy Spirit. Do not, therefore, offend matter:
it is not contemptible, because nothing that God has made
is contemptible. (Cf. *Contra imaginum calumniatores* I, 16,
ed. Kotter, pp. 89–90)

We see that as a result of the Incarnation, matter is seen to
have become divine, is seen as the habitation of God. It is
a new vision of the world and of material reality. God
became flesh, and flesh became truly the habitation of God,
whose glory shines in the human Face of Christ. Thus the
arguments of the Doctor of the East are still extremely
relevant today, considering the very great dignity that matter has acquired through the Incarnation, capable of becoming, through faith, a sign and a sacrament, efficacious in
the meeting of man with God. John Damascene remains,
therefore, a privileged witness of the cult of icons, which
would come to be one of the most distinctive aspects of
Eastern spirituality up to the present day. It is, however, a
form of cult which belongs simply to the Christian faith,
to the faith in that God who became flesh and was made

visible. The teaching of Saint John Damascene thus finds its place in the tradition of the universal Church, whose sacramental doctrine foresees that material elements taken from nature can become vehicles of grace by virtue of the invocation (*epiclesis*) of the Holy Spirit, accompanied by the confession of the true faith.

John Damascene extends these fundamental ideas to the veneration of the relics of Saints, on the basis of the conviction that the Christian Saints, having become partakers of the Resurrection of Christ, cannot be considered simply "dead". Numbering, for example, those whose relics or images are worthy of veneration, John states in his third discourse in defense of images:

> First of all (let us venerate) those among whom God reposed, he alone Holy, who reposes among the Saints (cf. Is 57:15), such as the Mother of God and all the Saints. These are those who, as far as possible, have made themselves similar to God by their own will; and by God's presence in them, and his help, they are really called gods (cf. Ps 82[81]:6), not by their nature, but by contingency, just as the red-hot iron is called fire, not by its nature, but by contingency and its participation in the fire. He says in fact: you shall be holy, because I am Holy (cf. Lv 19:2). (III, 33, 1352 A)

After a series of references of this kind, John Damascene was able serenely to deduce:

> God, who is good, and greater than any goodness, was not content with the contemplation of himself, but he desired that there should be beings benefited by him, who might share in his goodness: therefore he created from nothing all things, visible and invisible, including man, a reality visible and invisible. And he created him envisaging him and creating him as a being capable of thought (*ennoema ergon*), enriched

with the word (*logo [i] symploroumenon*), and orientated toward
the spirit (*pneumati teleioumenon*). (II, 2, PG 94, 865 A)

And to clarify this thought further, he adds: "We must allow
ourselves to be filled with wonder (*thaumazein*) at all the
works of Providence (*tes pronoias erga*), to accept and praise
them all, overcoming any temptation to identify in them
aspects which to many may seem unjust or iniquitous (*adika*)
and admitting instead that the project of God (*pronoia*) goes
beyond man's capacity to know or to understand (*agnoston
kai akatalepton*), while on the contrary only he may know
our thoughts, our actions, and even our future" (II, 29, *PG*
94, 964 C). Plato had in fact already said that all philosophy
begins with wonder. Our faith, too, begins with wonder at
the very fact of the Creation and at the beauty of God who
makes himself visible.

The optimism of the contemplation of nature (*physikè
theoria*), of seeing in the visible Creation the good, the beautiful, the true, this Christian optimism, is not ingenuous: it
takes account of the wound inflicted on human nature by
the freedom of choice desired by God and misused by man,
with all the consequences of widespread discord which have
derived from it. From this derives the need, clearly perceived by John Damascene, that nature, in which the goodness and beauty of God are reflected, wounded by our fault,
"should be strengthened and renewed" by the descent of
the Son of God in the flesh, after God had tried in many
ways and on many occasions to show that he had created
man so that he might exist not only in "being", but also in
"well-being" (cf. *The Orthodox Faith* II, 1, PG 94, 981).
With passionate eagerness John explains: "It was necessary
for nature to be strengthened and renewed and for the path
of virtue to be indicated and effectively taught (*didachthenai*

aretes hodòn), the path that leads away from corruption and toward eternal life. . . . So there appeared on the horizon of history the great sea of love that God bears toward man (*philanthropias pelagos*). . . ." It is a fine expression. We see on one side the beauty of Creation and, on the other, the destruction wrought by the fault of man. But we see in the Son of God, who descends to renew nature, the sea of love that God has for man. John Damascene continues: "he himself, the Creator and the Lord, fought for his Creation, transmitting to it his teaching by example. . . . And so the Son of God, while still remaining in the form of God, lowered the skies and descended . . . to his servants . . . achieving the newest thing of all, the only thing really new under the sun, through which he manifested the infinite power of God" (III, 1, *PG* 94, 981c–984b).

We may imagine the comfort and joy which these words, so rich in fascinating images, poured into the hearts of the faithful. We listen to them today, sharing the same feelings with the Christians of those far-off days: God desires to repose in us, he wishes to renew nature through our conversion, he wants to allow us to share in his divinity. May the Lord help us to make these words the substance of our lives.

17

Saint Theodore the Studite

WEDNESDAY, 27 MAY 2009
Saint Peter's Square

Dear Brothers and Sisters,

The Saint we meet today, Saint Theodore the Studite, brings us to the middle of the medieval Byzantine period, in a somewhat turbulent period from the religious and political perspectives. Saint Theodore was born in 759 into a devout noble family: his mother, Theoctista, and an uncle, Plato, Abbot of the Monastery of Saccudium in Bithynia, are venerated as Saints. Indeed, it was his uncle who guided him toward monastic life, which he embraced at the age of twenty-two. He was ordained a priest by Patriarch Tarasius, but he soon ended his relationship with him because of the toleration the Patriarch showed in the case of the adulterous marriage of Emperor Constantine VI. This led to Theodore's exile in 796 to Thessalonica. He was reconciled with the imperial authority the following year under the Empress Irene, whose benevolence induced Theodore and Plato to transfer to the urban monastery of Studios, together with a large portion of the community of the monks of Saccudium, in order to avoid the Saracen incursions. So it was that the important "Studite Reform" began.

Theodore's personal life, however, continued to be eventful. With his usual energy, he became the leader of the resistance against the iconoclasm of Leo V, the Armenian who once again opposed the existence of images and icons in the Church. The procession of icons organized by the monks of Studios evoked a reaction from the police. Between 815 and 821, Theodore was scourged, imprisoned, and exiled to various places in Asia Minor. In the end he was able to return to Constantinople but not to his own monastery. He therefore settled with his monks on the other side of the Bosporus. He is believed to have died in Prinkipo on 11 November 826, the day on which he is commemorated in the Byzantine Calendar. Theodore distinguished himself within Church history as one of the great reformers of monastic life and as a defender of the veneration of sacred images, beside Saint Nicephorus, Patriarch of Constantinople, in the second phase of iconoclasm. Theodore had realized that the issue of the veneration of icons was calling into question the truth of the Incarnation itself. In his three books, the *Antirretikoi* (*Confutations*), Theodore makes a comparison between eternal intra-Trinitarian relations, in which the existence of each of the divine Persons does not destroy their unity, and the relations between Christ's two natures, which do not jeopardize in him the one Person of the *Logos*. He also argues: abolishing veneration of the icon of Christ would mean repudiating his redeeming work, given that, in assuming human nature, the invisible eternal *Word* appeared in visible human flesh and in so doing sanctified the entire visible cosmos.

Theodore and his monks, courageous witnesses in the period of the Iconoclastic persecutions, were inseparably bound to the reform of coenobitic life in the Byzantine world. Their importance was notable if only for an external circumstance: their number. Whereas the number of monks in monasteries of that time did not exceed thirty or forty, we know from the *Life of Theodore* of the existence of more than one thousand Studite monks overall. Theodore himself tells us of the presence in his monastery of about three hundred monks; thus we see the enthusiasm of faith that was born within the context of this man's being truly informed and formed by faith itself. However, more influential than these numbers was the new spirit the Founder impressed on coenobitic life. In his writings, he insists on the urgent need for a conscious return to the teaching of the Fathers, especially to Saint Basil, the first legislator of monastic life, and to Saint Dorotheus of Gaza, a famous spiritual Father of the Palestinian desert. Theodore's characteristic contribution consists in insistence on the need for order and submission on the monks' part. During the persecutions they had scattered, and each one had grown accustomed to living according to his own judgment. Then, as it was possible to re-establish community life, it was necessary to do the utmost to make the monastery once again an organic community, a true family, or, as Saint Theodore said, a true "Body of Christ". In such a community the reality of the Church as a whole is realized concretely.

Another of Saint Theodore's basic convictions was this: monks, differently from lay people, take on the commitment to observe the Christian duties with greater strictness and intensity. For this reason they make a special profession which belongs to the *hagiasmata* (*consecrations*), and it is, as it were, a "new Baptism", symbolized by their taking the habit. Characteristic of monks in comparison with lay people, then, is the commitment to poverty, chastity, and obedience. In addressing his monks, Theodore spoke in a practical, at times picturesque manner about poverty, but poverty in the following of Christ is from the start an essential element of

monasticism and also points out a way for all of us. The
renunciation of private property, this freedom from material
things, as well as moderation and simplicity apply in a radical form only to monks, but the spirit of this renounce-
ment is equal for all. Indeed, we must not depend on material
possessions but instead must learn renunciation, simplicity,
austerity, and moderation. Only in this way can a supportive
society develop and the great problem of poverty in this world
be overcome. Therefore, in this regard the monks' radical
poverty is essentially also a path for us all. Then when he
explains the temptations against chastity, Theodore does not
conceal his own experience and indicates the way of inner
combat to find self-control and, hence, respect for one's own
body and for the body of the other as a temple of God.

However, the most important renunciations in his opinion are those required by obedience, because each one of
the monks has his own way of living, and fitting into the
large community of three hundred monks truly involves a
new way of life, which he describes as the "martyrdom of
submission". Here, too, the monks' example serves to show
us how necessary this is for us, because, after the original
sin, man has tended to do what he likes; the first principle
is the life of the world; all the rest must be subjected to
one's own will. However, in this way, if each person is self-
centered, the social structure cannot function. Only by learning to fit into the common freedom, to share and to submit
to it, learning legality, that is, submission and obedience to
the rules of the common good and life in common, can
society, as well as the *self*, be healed of the pride of being
the center of the world. Thus Saint Theodore, with fine
introspection, helped his monks and ultimately also helps
us to understand true life, to resist the temptation to set up
our own will as the supreme rule of life, and to preserve

our true personal identity—which is always an identity shared with others—and peace of heart.

For Theodore the Studite, an important virtue on a par with obedience and humility is *philergia*, that is, the love of work, in which he sees a criterion by which to judge the quality of personal devotion: the person who is fervent and works hard in material concerns, he argues, will be the same in those of the spirit. Therefore he does not permit the monk to dispense with work, including manual work, under the pretext of prayer and contemplation; for work to his mind and in the whole monastic tradition is actually a means of finding God. Theodore is not afraid to speak of work as the "sacrifice of the monk", as his "liturgy", even as a sort of Mass through which monastic life becomes angelic life. And it is precisely in this way that the world of work must be humanized and man, through work, becomes more himself and closer to God. One consequence of this unusual vision is worth remembering: precisely because it is the fruit of a form of "liturgy", the riches obtained from common work must not serve for the monks' comfort but must be earmarked for assistance to the poor. Here we can all understand the need for the proceeds of work to be a good for all. Obviously the "Studites'" work was not only manual: they had great importance in the religious and cultural development of the Byzantine civilization as calligraphers, painters, poets, educators of youth, school teachers, and librarians.

Although he exercised external activities on a truly vast scale, Theodore did not let himself be distracted from what he considered closely relevant to his role as superior: being the spiritual father of his monks. He knew what a crucial influence both his good mother and his holy uncle Plato, whom he described with the significant title "father", had had on his life. Thus he himself provided spiritual direction for the monks. Every day, his biographer says, after evening prayer he would place himself in front of the iconostasis to listen to the confidences of all. He also gave spiritual advice to many people outside the monastery. The *Spiritual Testament* and the *Letters* highlight his open and affectionate character and show that true spiritual friendships were born from his fatherhood both in the monastic context and outside it.

The *Rule*, known by the name of *Hypotyposis*, codified shortly after Theodore's death, was adopted, with a few modifications, on Mount Athos, when in 962 Saint Athanasius Athonite founded the Great Laura there, and in the Kievan Rus', when at the beginning of the second millennium Saint Theodosius introduced it into the Laura of the Grottos. Understood in its genuine meaning, the *Rule* has proven to be unusually up to date. Numerous trends today threaten the unity of the common faith and impel people toward a sort of dangerous spiritual individualism and spiritual pride. It is necessary to strive to defend and to increase the perfect unity of the Body of Christ, in which the peace of order and sincere personal relations in the Spirit harmoniously consist.

It may be useful to return at the end to some of the main elements of Theodore's spiritual doctrine: love for the Lord incarnate and for his visibility in the liturgy and in icons; fidelity to Baptism and the commitment to live in communion with the Body of Christ, also understood as the communion of Christians with each other; a spirit of poverty, moderation, and renunciation; chastity, self-control, humility, and obedience against the primacy of one's own will that destroys the social fabric and the peace of souls; love for physical and spiritual work; spiritual love born from the purification of one's own conscience, one's own soul, one's own life. Let us seek to comply with these teachings, which really do show us the path of true life.

18

Rabanus Maurus

Dear Brothers and Sisters,

Today I would like to speak of a truly extraordinary figure of the Latin West: Rabanus Maurus, a monk. Together with men such as Isidore of Seville, the Venerable Bede, and Ambrose Autpert, of whom I have already spoken in previous Cate-cheses, during the centuries of the so-called "High Middle Ages" he was able to preserve contact with the great culture of the ancient scholars and of the Christian Fathers. Often remembered as the "*praeceptor Germaniae*", Rabanus Maurus was extraordinarily prolific. With his absolutely exceptional capacity for work, he perhaps made a greater contribution than anyone else to keeping alive that theological, exegetic, and spiritual culture on which successive centuries were to draw. He was referred to by great figures belonging to the monastic world, such as Peter Damian, Peter the Venerable, and Bernard of Clairvaux, as well as by an ever-increasing number of "*clerics*" of the secular clergy, who in the twelfth and thirteenth centuries gave life to one of the most beautiful periods of the fruitful flourishing of human thought.

Born in Mainz in about 780, Rabanus entered the mon-astery at a very early age. He was surnamed "Maurus" after the young Saint Maur, who, according to *Book II of the Dialogues* of Saint Gregory the Great, was entrusted by his parents, Roman nobles, to the Abbot Benedict of Norcia. This precocious insertion of Rabanus as *"puer oblatus"* in the Benedictine monastic world and the benefits he drew from it for his own human, cultural, and spiritual growth were in themselves to provide an interesting glimpse not only of the life of monks and of the Church, but also of the whole of society of his time, usually described as "Carolingian". About them or perhaps about himself, Rabanus Maurus wrote: "There are some who have had the good fortune to be introduced to the knowledge of Scripture from a tender age (*"a cunabulis suis"*) and who were so well-nourished with the food offered to them by Holy Church as to be fit for promotion, with the appropriate training, to the highest of sacred Orders" (*PL* 107, 419 BC).

The extraordinary culture for which Rabanus Maurus was distinguished soon brought him to the attention of the great of his time. He became the advisor of princes. He strove to guarantee the unity of the Empire and, at a broader cultural level, never refused to give those who questioned him a carefully considered reply, which he found preferably in the Bible or in the texts of the Holy Fathers. First elected Abbot of the famous Monastery of Fulda and then appointed Archbishop of Mainz, his native city, he did not cease to pursue his studies, showing by the example of his life that it is possible to be at the same time available to others without depriving oneself of the appropriate time for reflection, study, and meditation. Thus Rabanus Maurus was exegete, philosopher, poet, pastor, and man of God. The Dioceses of Fulda, Mainz, Limburg, and Breslau (Wrocław) venerate him as a Saint or Blessed. His works fill at least six volumes of Migne's *Patrologia Latina*. It is likely that we are indebted to him for one of the most beautiful hymns known to the Latin Church, the "*Veni Creator Spiritus*", an extraordinary synthesis of Christian pneumatology. In fact, Rabanus' first theological work is expressed in the form of poetry and had as its subject the mystery of the Holy Cross in a book entitled: *De laudibus Sanctae Crucis*, conceived in such a way as to suggest not only a conceptual content but also more exquisitely artistic stimuli, by the use of both poetic and pictorial forms within the same manuscript codex. Suggesting the image of the Crucified Christ between the lines of his writing, he says, for example: "This is the image of the Savior who, with the position of his limbs, makes sacred for us the most salubrious, gentle, and loving form of the Cross, so that by believing in his Name and obeying his commandments we may obtain eternal life thanks to his Passion. However, every time we raise our eyes to the Cross, let us remember the one who died for us to save us from the powers of darkness, accepting death to make us heirs to eternal life" (*Lib.* I, fig. I: *PL* 107, 151 C).

This method of combining all the arts, the intellect, the heart, and the senses, which came from the East, was to experience a great development in the West, reaching unparalleled heights in the miniature codices of the Bible and in other works of faith and art that flourished in Europe until the invention of printing and beyond. In Rabanus Maurus, in any case, is shown an extraordinary awareness of the need to involve, in the experience of faith, not only the mind and the heart, but also the senses through those other aspects of aesthetic taste and human sensitivity that lead man to benefit from the truth with his whole self, "mind, soul, and body". This is important: faith is not only thought but also touches the whole of our being. Since God became man in flesh and blood, since he entered the tangible world, we must seek and encounter God in all the dimensions of our being. Thus the reality of God, through faith, penetrates our being and transforms it. This is why Rabanus Maurus focused his attention above all on the liturgy as a synthesis of all the dimensions of our perception of reality. This intuition of Rabanus Maurus makes him extraordinarily up to date. Also famous among his works are the "*Hymns*", suggested for use especially in liturgical celebrations. In fact, since Rabanus was primarily a monk, his interest in the liturgical celebration was taken for granted. However, he did not devote himself to the art of poetry as an end in itself but, rather, used art and every other form of erudition as a means for deepening knowledge of the Word of God. He therefore sought with great application and rigor to introduce his contemporaries, especially ministers (Bishops, priests, and deacons), to an understanding of the profoundly theological and spiritual meaning of all the elements of the liturgical celebration.

He thus sought to understand and to present to others the theological meanings concealed in the rites, drawing from the Bible and from the tradition of the Fathers. For the sake of honesty and to give greater weight to his explanations, he did not hesitate to indicate the Patristic sources to which he owed his knowledge. Nevertheless, he used them with freedom and with careful discernment, continuing the development of Patristic thought. At the end of the "*Epistula prima*", addressed to a "chorbishop" of the Diocese of Mainz, for example, after answering the requests for clarification concerning the behavior to adopt in the exercise of pastoral responsibility, he continues, "We have written all these things for you as we deduced them from the Sacred Scriptures and the canons of the Fathers. Yet, most holy man, may you take your decisions as you think best, case by case, seeking to temper your evaluation in such a way as to guarantee discretion in all things because it is the mother of all the virtues" (*Epistulae* I: *PL* 112, 1510 C). Thus the continuity of the Christian faith which originates in the Word of God becomes visible; yet it is always alive, develops, and is expressed in new ways, ever consistent with the whole construction, with the whole edifice of faith.

Since an integral part of liturgical celebration is the Word of God, Rabanus Maurus dedicated himself to it with the greatest commitment throughout his life. He produced appropriate exegetic explanations for almost all the biblical books of the Old and New Testament, with clearly pastoral intentions that he justified with words such as these: "I have written these things .. summing up the explanations and suggestions of many others, not only in order to offer a service to the poor reader, who may not have many books at his disposal, but also to make it easier for those who in many things do not succeed in entering in depth into an understanding of the meanings discovered by the Fathers" (*Commentariorum in Matthaeum praefatio*: *PL* 107, 727 D). In fact, in commenting on the biblical texts he drew amply from the ancient Fathers, with special preference for Jerome, Ambrose, Augustine, and Gregory the Great.

His outstanding pastoral sensitivity later led him to occupy himself above all with one of the problems most acutely felt by the faithful and sacred ministers of his time: that of penance. Indeed, he compiled the *"Penitenziari"*—this is what he called them—in which, according to the sensibility of his day, sins and the corresponding punishments were listed, using as far as possible reasons found in the Bible, in the decisions of the Councils, and in Papal Decretals. The "Carolingians" also used these texts in their attempt to reform the Church and society. Corresponding with the same pastoral intentions were works such as "*De disciplina ecclesiastica*" and "*De institutione clericorum*", in which, drawing above all from Augustine, Rabanus explained to the simple and to the clergy of his diocese the basic elements of the Christian faith: they were like little catechisms.

I would like to end the presentation of this great "churchman" by quoting some of his words in which his basic conviction is clearly reflected: "Those who are negligent in contemplation ("*qui vacare Deo negligit*"), deprive themselves of the vision of God's light; then those who let themselves be indiscreetly invaded by worries and allow their thoughts to be overwhelmed by the tumult of worldly things condemn themselves to the absolute impossibility of penetrating the secrets of the invisible God" (*Lib* I: *PL* 112, 1263 A). I think that Rabanus Maurus is also addressing these words to us today: in periods of work, with its frenetic pace, and in holiday periods we must reserve moments for God. We must open our lives to him, addressing to him a thought, a reflection, a brief prayer, and above all we must not forget Sunday as the Lord's Day, the day of the liturgy, in order to perceive God's beauty itself in the beauty of our churches, in our sacred music, and in the Word of God, letting him enter our being. Only in this way does our life become great, become true life.

19

John Scotus Erigena

Dear Brothers and Sisters,

Today I would like to speak of a noteworthy thinker of the Christian West: John Scotus Erigena, whose origins are nonetheless obscure. He certainly came from Ireland, where he was born at the beginning of the ninth century, but we do not know when he left his Island to cross the Channel and thus fully enter that cultural world which was coming into being around the Carolingians, and in particular around Charles the Bald, in ninth-century France. Just as we are not certain of the date of his birth, likewise we do not know the year of his death, but, according to the experts, it must have been in about the year 870.

John Scotus Erigena had a Patristic education, both Greek and Latin, at first hand. Indeed, he had direct knowledge of the writings of both the Latin and the Greek Fathers. He was well acquainted, among others, with the works of Augustine, Ambrose, Gregory the Great, and the important Fathers of the Christian West, but he was just as familiar with the thought of Origen, Gregory of Nyssa, John Chrysostom, and other Christian Fathers of the East who were equally important. In that period, it was an exceptional man who mastered the Greek language as well. He devoted very special attention to Saint Maximus Confessor and above all to Dionysius the Areopagite. This pseudonym conceals a fifth-century ecclesiastical writer, but throughout the Middle Ages people, including John Scotus Erigena, were convinced that this author could be identified with a direct disciple of Saint Paul who is mentioned in the Acts of the Apostles (17:34). Scotus Erigena, convinced of the apostolicity of Dionysius' writings, described him as a "divine author" par excellence; Dionysius' writings were therefore an eminent source of his thought. John Scotus translated his works into Latin. The great medieval theologians, such as Saint Bonaventure, became acquainted with Dionysius' works through this translation. Throughout his life John Scotus devoted himself to deepening his knowledge and developing his thought, drawing on these writings, to the point that still today it can sometimes be difficult to distinguish where we are dealing with Scotus Erigena's thought and where, instead, he is merely proposing anew the thought of Pseudo-Dionysius.

The theological opus of John Scotus truly did not meet with much favor. Not only did the end of the Carolingian era cause his works to be forgotten; a censure on the part of Church authorities also cast a shadow over him. In fact, John Scotus represents a radical Platonism that sometimes seems to approach a pantheistic vision, even though his personal subjective intentions were always orthodox. Some of John Scotus Erigena's works have come down to us, among which the following in particular deserve mention: the Treatise "On the Division of Nature" and the expositions on "The Heavenly Hierarchy" of Saint Dionysius. In them he continues to develop stimulating theological and spiritual reflections which could suggest an interesting furthering of knowledge also to contemporary theologians. I refer, for example, to what he wrote on the duty of exercising an appropriate discernment on what is presented as *auctoritas vera*, or on the commitment to continue the quest for the truth until one achieves some experience of it in the silent adoration of God.

Our author says: "*Salus nostra ex fide inchoat:* our salvation begins with faith"; in other words, we cannot speak of God starting with our own inventions, but rather we must start with what God says of himself in the Sacred Scriptures. Since, however, God tells only the truth, Scotus Erigena is convinced that authority and reason can never contradict each other; he is convinced that true religion and true philosophy coincide. In this perspective he writes: "Any type of authority that is not confirmed by true reason must be considered weak. . . . Indeed, there is no true authority other than that which coincides with the truth, discovered by virtue of reason, even should one be dealing with an authority recommended and handed down for the use of the successors of the holy Fathers" (I: *PL* 122, 513 BC). Consequently, he warns: "Let no authority intimidate you or distract you from what makes you understand the conviction obtained through correct rational contemplation. Indeed, the authentic authority never contradicts right reason, nor can the latter ever contradict a true authority. "The one and the other both come indisputably from the same source, which is divine wisdom" (I: *PL* 122, 511 B). We see here a brave affirmation of the value of reason, founded on the certainty that the true authority is reasonable, because God is creative reason.

According to Erigena, Scripture itself does not escape the need to be approached with the same criterion of discernment. In fact, although Scripture comes from God— the Irish theologian maintains, proposing anew a reflection

made earlier by John Chrysostom—it would not be necessary had the human being not sinned. It must therefore be
deduced that Scripture was given by God with a pedagog-
ical intention and with indulgence so that man might remember all that had been impressed within his heart from the
moment of his creation, "in the image and likeness of God"
(cf. Gn 1:26), and that the Fall of man had caused him to
forget. Erigena writes in his *Expositiones:* "It is not man
who was created for Scripture, which he would not have
needed had he not sinned, but rather it is Scripture, interwoven with doctrine and symbols, which was given to man.
Thanks to Scripture, in fact, our rational nature may be
introduced to the secrets of authentic and pure contemplation of God" (II: *PL* 122, 146 C). The words of Sacred
Scripture purify our somewhat blind reason and help us to
recover the memory of what we, as the image of God, carry
in our hearts, unfortunately wounded by sin.

From this derive certain hermeneutical consequences concerning the way to interpret Scripture that still today can
point out the right approach for a correct reading of Sacred
Scripture. In fact, it is a question of discovering the hidden
meaning in the Sacred Text, and this implies a special inner
exercise through which reason is open to the sure road to
the truth. This exercise consists in cultivating constant readi-
ness for conversion. Indeed, to acquire an in-depth vision of
the text, it is necessary to progress at the same time in conversion of the heart and in the conceptual analysis of the
biblical passage, whether it is of a cosmic, historical, or doctrinal character. Indeed, it is only by means of a constant
purification of both the eye of the heart and the eye of the
mind that it is possible to arrive at an exact understanding.

This arduous, demanding, and exciting journey, which
consists of continuous achievements and the relativization

of human knowledge, leads the intelligent creature to the threshold of the divine Mystery, where all notions admit of their own weakness and inability and thus, with the simple free and sweet power of the truth, make it obligatory ceaselessly to surpass all that is progressively achieved. Worshipful and silent recognition of the Mystery which flows into unifying communion is therefore revealed as the only path to a relationship with the truth that is at the same time the most intimate possible and the most scrupulously respectful of otherness. John Scotus, here too using terminology dear to the Christian tradition of the Greek language, called this experience for which we strive "theosis", or divinization, with such daring affirmations that he might be suspected of heterodox pantheism. Yet, even today one cannot but be strongly moved by texts such as the following in which—with recourse to the ancient metaphor of the smelting of iron—he writes: "just as all red-hot iron is liquified to the point that it seems nothing but fire and yet the substances remain distinct from one another, so it must be accepted that after the end of this world all nature, both the corporeal and the incorporeal, will show forth God alone and yet remain integral so that God can in a certain way be com-prehended while remaining in-comprehensible and that the creature itself may be transformed, with ineffable wonder, and reunited with God" (V: *PL* 122, 451 B).

In fact, the entire theological thought of John Scotus is the most evident demonstration of the attempt to express the expressible of the inexpressible God, based solely upon the mystery of the Word made flesh in Jesus of Nazareth. The numerous metaphors John Scotus used to point out this ineffable reality show how aware he was of the absolute inadequacy of the terms in which we speak of these things.

And yet the enchantment and that aura of authentic mystical experience, which every now and then one can feel tangibly in his texts, endure. As proof of this, it suffices to cite a passage from *De divisione naturae* which deeply touches even the minds of us twenty-first-century believers: "We should desire nothing", he writes, "other than the joy of the truth that is Christ, avoid nothing other than his absence. The greatest torment of a rational creature consists in the deprivation or absence of Christ. Indeed, this must be considered the one cause of total and eternal sorrow. Take Christ from me, and I am left with no good thing, nor will anything terrify me so much as his absence. The greatest torments of a rational creature are the deprivation and absence of him" (V: *PL* 122, 989 A). These are words that we can make our own, translating them into a prayer to the One for whom our hearts long.

20

Saints Cyril and Methodius

WEDNESDAY, 17 JUNE 2009
Saint Peter's Square

Dear Brothers and Sisters,

Today I would like to talk about Saints Cyril and Methodius, brothers by blood and in the faith, the so-called "Apostles to the Slavs". Cyril was born in Thessalonica to Leo, an imperial magistrate, in 826 or 827. He was the youngest of seven. As a child he learned the Slavonic language. When he was fourteen years old, he was sent to Constantinople to be educated and was companion to the young Emperor, Michael III. In those years Cyril was introduced to the various university disciplines, including dialectics, and his teacher was Photius. After refusing a brilliant marriage, he decided to receive holy Orders and became "librarian" at the Patriarchate. Shortly afterward, wishing to retire in solitude, he went into hiding at a monastery but was soon discovered and entrusted with teaching the sacred and profane sciences. He carried out this office so well that he earned the title of "Philosopher". In the meantime, his brother Michael (born in about 815) left the world after an administrative career in Macedonia and withdrew to a monastic life on Mount Olympus in Bithynia, where he was given the name "Methodius" (a monk's monastic name had to begin with the same letter as his baptismal name) and became hegumen of the Monastery of Polychron.

Attracted by his brother's example, Cyril, too, decided to give up teaching and go to Mount Olympus to meditate and pray. A few years later (in about 861), the imperial government sent him on a mission to the Khazars on the Sea of Azov, who had asked for a scholar to be sent to them who could converse with both Jews and Saracens. Cyril, accompanied by his brother Methodius, stayed for a long time in Crimea, where he learned Hebrew and sought the body of Pope Clement I, who had been exiled there. Cyril found Pope Clement's tomb, and, when he made the return journey with his brother, he took Clement's precious relics with him. Having arrived in Constantinople, the two brothers were sent to Moravia by Emperor Michael III, who had received a specific request from Prince Ratislav of Moravia: "Since our people rejected paganism," Ratislav wrote to Michael, "they have embraced the Christian law; but we do not have a teacher who can explain the true faith to us in our own language." The mission was soon unusually successful. By translating the liturgy into the Slavonic language, the two brothers earned immense popularity.

However, this gave rise to hostility among the Frankish clergy who had arrived in Moravia before the brothers and considered the territory to be under their ecclesiastical jurisdiction. In order to justify themselves, in 867 the two brothers traveled to Rome. On the way they stopped in Venice, where they had a heated discussion with the champions of the so-called "trilingual heresy", who claimed that there were only three languages in which it was lawful to praise God: Hebrew, Greek, and Latin. The two brothers obviously forcefully opposed this claim. In Rome Cyril and Methodius were received by Pope Adrian II, who led a

procession to meet them in order to give a dignified welcome to Saint Clement's relics. The Pope had also realized
the great importance of their exceptional mission. Since the
middle of the first millennium, in fact, thousands of Slavs
had settled in those territories located between the two parts
of the Roman Empire, the East and the West, whose relations were fraught with tension. The Pope perceived that
the Slav peoples would be able to serve as a bridge and
thereby help to preserve the union between the Christians
of both parts of the Empire. Thus he did not hesitate to
approve the mission of the two brothers in Great Moravia,
accepting and approving the use of the Slavonic language
in the liturgy. The Slavonic Books were laid on the altar of
Saint Mary of Phatmé (Saint Mary Major), and the liturgy
in the Slavonic tongue was celebrated in the Basilicas of
Saint Peter, Saint Andrew, and Saint Paul.

Unfortunately, Cyril fell seriously ill in Rome. Feeling
that his death was at hand, he wanted to consecrate himself totally to God as a monk in one of the Greek monasteries of the City (probably Santa Prassede) and took the
monastic name of Cyril (his baptismal name was Constantine). He then insistently begged his brother Methodius,
who in the meantime had been ordained a Bishop, not to
abandon their mission in Moravia and to return to the
peoples there. He addressed this prayer to God: "Lord, my
God, ... hear my prayers and keep the flock you have
entrusted to me faithful. . . . Free them from the heresy of
the three languages, gather them all in unity, and make
the people you have chosen agree in the true faith and
confession." He died on 14 February 869.

Faithful to the pledge he had made with his brother, Methodius returned to Moravia and Pannonia (today, Hungary)
the following year, 870, where once again he encountered

the violent aversion of the Frankish missionaries, who took
him prisoner. He did not lose heart, and when he was
released in 873, he worked hard to organize the Church
and train a group of disciples. It was to the merit of these
disciples that it was possible to survive the crisis unleashed
after the death of Methodius on 6 April 885: persecuted
and imprisoned, some of them were sold as slaves and taken
to Venice, where they were redeemed by a Constantino-
politan official, who allowed them to return to the countries of the Slavonic Balkans. Welcomed in Bulgaria, they
were able to continue the mission that Methodius had begun
and to disseminate the Gospel in the "Land of the Rus".
God with his mysterious Providence thus availed himself of
their persecution to save the work of the holy brothers.
Literary documentation of their work is extant. It suffices
to think of texts such as the *Evangeliarium* (liturgical passages of the New Testament), the *Psalter*, various *liturgical
texts* in Slavonic, on which both the brothers had worked.
Indeed, after Cyril's death, it is to Methodius and to his
disciples that we owe the translation of the entire *Sacred
Scriptures*, the *Nomocanone*, and the *Book of the Fathers*.

Wishing now to sum up concisely the profile of the two
brothers, we should first recall the enthusiasm with which
Cyril approached the writings of Saint Gregory Nazianzen,
learning from him the value of language in the transmis-
sion of Revelation. Saint Gregory had expressed the wish
that Christ would speak through him: "I am a servant of
the Word, so I put myself at the service of the Word." Desir-
ous of imitating Gregory in this service, Cyril asked Christ
to deign to speak in Slavonic through him. He introduced
his work of translation with the solemn invocation: "Listen,
O all of you Slav Peoples, listen to the word that comes
from God, the word that nourishes souls, the word that

leads to the knowledge of God." In fact, a few years before the Prince of Moravia had asked Emperor Michael III to send missionaries to his country, it seems that Cyril and his brother Methodius, surrounded by a group of disciples, were already working on the project of collecting the Christian dogmas in books written in Slavonic. The need for new graphic characters closer to the language spoken was therefore clearly apparent: so it was that the Glagolitic alphabet came into being. Subsequently modified, it was later designated by the name "Cyrillic", in honor of the man who inspired it. It was a crucial event for the development of the Slav civilization in general. Cyril and Methodius were convinced that the individual peoples could not claim to have received Revelation fully unless they had heard it in their own language and read it in the characters proper to their own alphabet.

Methodius had the merit of ensuring that the work begun by his brother was not suddenly interrupted. While Cyril, the "Philosopher", was more inclined to contemplation, Methodius, on the other hand, had a leaning for the active life. Thanks to this he was able to lay the foundations of the successive affirmation of what we might call the "Cyrillian-Methodian idea": it accompanied the Slav peoples in the different periods of their history, encouraging their cultural, national, and religious development. This was already recognized by Pope Pius XI in his Apostolic Letter *Quod Sanctum Cyrillum*, in which he described the two brothers: "Sons of the East, Byzantines according to their homeland, Greeks by birth, Romans by their mission, Slavs by their apostolic fruit" (*AAS* 19 [1927] 93–96). The historic role they played was later officially proclaimed by Pope John Paul II, who, with his Apostolic Letter *Egregiae Virtutis*, declared them Co-Patrons of Europe, together with

Saint Benedict (31 December 1980; *L'Osservatore Romano* English edition, 19 January 1981, p. 3). Cyril and Methodius are in fact a classic example of what today is meant by the term "inculturation": every people must integrate the message revealed into its own culture and express its saving truth in its own language. This implies a very demanding effort of "translation", because it requires the identification of the appropriate words to present anew, without distortion, the riches of the revealed Word. The two holy brothers have left us a most important testimony of this, to which the Church also looks today in order to draw from it inspiration and guidelines.

21

Saint Odo of Cluny

WEDNESDAY, 2 SEPTEMBER 2009
Paul VI Audience Hall

Dear Brothers and Sisters,

After a long pause, I would like to resume the presentation of important writers of the Eastern and Western Church in the Middle Ages because in their life and writings we see as in a mirror what it means to be Christian. Today I present to you the luminous figure of Saint Odo, Abbot of Cluny. He fits into that period of medieval monasticism which saw the surprising success in Europe of the life and spirituality inspired by the *Rule of Saint Benedict*. In those centuries there was a wonderful increase in the number of cloisters that sprang up and branched out over the Continent, spreading the Christian spirit and sensibility far and wide. Saint Odo takes us back in particular to Cluny, one of the most illustrious and famous monasteries in the Middle Ages that still today reveals to us, through its majestic ruins, the signs of a past rendered glorious by intense dedication to ascesis, study, and, in a special way, to divine worship, endowed with decorum and beauty.

Odo was the second Abbot of Cluny. He was born in about 880, on the boundary between the Maine and the Touraine regions of France. Odo's father consecrated him

to the holy Bishop Martin of Tours, in whose beneficent
shadow and memory he was to spend his entire life, which
he ended close to Saint Martin's tomb. His choice of religious consecration was preceded by the inner experience
of a special moment of grace, of which he himself spoke to
another monk, John the Italian, who later became his biographer. Odo was still an adolescent, about sixteen years old,
when one Christmas Eve he felt this prayer to the Virgin
rise spontaneously to his lips: "My Lady, Mother of Mercy,
who on this night gave birth to the Savior, pray for me.
May your glorious and unique experience of childbirth, O
Most Devout Mother, be my refuge" (*Vita sancti Odonis* I,
9: *PL* 133, 747). The name "Mother of Mercy", with which
young Odo then invoked the Virgin, was to be the title by
which he always subsequently liked to address Mary. He
also called her "the one Hope of the world ... thanks to
whom the gates of Heaven were opened to us" (*In venera-
tione S. Mariae Magdalenae: PL* 133, 721). At that time Odo
chanced to come across the *Rule of Saint Benedict* and to
comment on it, "bearing, while not yet a monk, the light
yoke of monks" (*ibid.*, I, 14: *PL* 133, 50). In one of his
sermons Odo was to celebrate Benedict as the "lamp that
shines in the dark period of life" (*De sancto Benedicto abbate:
PL* 133, 725) and to describe him as "a teacher of spiritual
discipline" (*ibid.: PL* 133, 727). He was to point out with
affection that Christian piety, "with the liveliest gentleness
commemorates him" in the knowledge that God raised him
"among the supreme and elect Fathers of Holy Church"
(*ibid.: PL* 133, 722).

Fascinated by the Benedictine ideal, Odo left Tours and
entered the Benedictine Abbey of Baume as a monk; he
later moved to Cluny, of which in 927 he became Abbot.
From that center of spiritual life he was able to exercise a

vast influence over the monasteries on the Continent. Various monasteries or coenobia were able to benefit from his guidance and reform, including that of Saint Paul Outside-the-Walls. More than once Odo visited Rome, and he even went as far as Subiaco, Monte Cassino, and Salerno. He was in fact in Rome when he fell ill in the summer of 942. Feeling that he was nearing his end, he wanted with all his might to return to Saint Martin in Tours, where he died, in the Octave of the Saint's feast, on 18 November 942. His biographer, stressing the "virtue of patience" that Odo possessed, gives a long list of his other virtues that include contempt of the world, zeal for souls, and the commitment to peace in the Churches. Abbot Odo's great aspirations were: concord between kings and princes, the observance of the commandments, attention to the poor, the correction of youth, and respect for the elderly (cf. *Vita sancti Odonis* I, 17: *PL* 133, 49).

He loved the cell in which he dwelled, "removed from the eyes of all, eager to please God alone" (*ibid.*, I, 14: *PL* 133, 49). However, he did not fail also to exercise, as a "superabundant source", the ministry of the word and to set an example, "regretting the immense wretchedness of this world" (*ibid.*, I, 17: *PL* 133, 51). In a single monk, his biographer comments, were united the various virtues that, in other monasteries, exist only few and far between: "Jesus, in his goodness, drawing on the various gardens of monks, in a small space created a paradise, in order to water the hearts of the faithful from its fountains" (*ibid.*, I, 14: *PL* 133, 49). In a passage from a sermon in honor of Mary of Magdala, the Abbot of Cluny reveals to us how he conceived of monastic life: "Mary, who, seated at the Lord's feet, listened attentively to his words, is the symbol of the sweetness of contemplative life; the more its savor is tasted, the more it induces

the mind to be detached from visible things and the tumult
of the world's preoccupations" (*In ven. S. Mariae Magd.*: *PL*
133, 717). Odo strengthened and developed this conception
in his other writings, through which his love for interiority
shines along with a vision of the world as a brittle, precarious reality from which to uproot oneself, a constant incli-
nation to detachment from things felt to be sources of anxiety,
an acute sensitivity to the presence of evil in the various
types of people, and a deep eschatological aspiration. This
vision of the world may appear rather distant from our own;
yet Odo's conception of it, his perception of the fragility of
the world, brings out the value of an inner life that is open
to the other, to the love of one's neighbor, and in this very
way transforms life and opens the world to God's light.

Deserving of special mention is the "devotion" to the Body
and Blood of Christ that Odo, faced with a widespread neglect
of them that he himself deeply deplored, always cultivated
with conviction. Odo was in fact firmly convinced of the
Real Presence, under the Eucharistic species, of the Body
and Blood of the Lord, by virtue of the conversion of the
"substance" of the bread and the wine. He wrote: "God,
Creator of all things, took the bread saying that this was his
Body and that he would offer it for the world, and he distributed the wine, calling it his Blood"; now, "it is a law of
nature that the change should come about in accordance
with the Creator's command", and thus "nature immediately changes its usual condition: the bread instantly becomes
flesh, and the wine becomes blood"; at the Lord's order,
"the substance changes" (*Odonis Abb. Cluniac. occupatio*, ed.
A. Swoboda, Leipzig, 1900, p. 121). Unfortunately, our Abbot
notes, this "sacrosanct mystery of the Lord's Body, in whom
the whole salvation of the world consists" (*Collationes* XXVIII:
PL 133, 572), is celebrated carelessly. "Priests", he warns,

"who approach the altar unworthily stain the bread, that is, the Body of Christ" (*ibid.: PL* 133, 572–573). Only those who are spiritually united to Christ may worthily share in his Eucharistic Body: should the contrary be the case, to eat his Flesh and to drink his Blood would not be beneficial but rather a condemnation (cf. *ibid.*, XXX: *PL* 133, 575). All this invites us to believe the truth of the Lord's presence with new force and depth. The presence in our midst of the Creator, who gives himself into our hands and transforms us as he transforms the bread and the wine, thus transforms the world.

Saint Odo was a true spiritual guide both for the monks and for the faithful of his time. In the face of the "immensity of the vices" widespread in society, the remedy he strongly advised was that of a radical change of life, based on humility, austerity, detachment from ephemeral things, and adherence to those that are eternal (cf. *Collationes* XXX: *PL* 133, 613). In spite of the realism of his diagnosis on the situation of his time, Odo does not indulge in pessimism: "We do not say this", he explains, "in order to plunge those who wish to convert into despair. Divine mercy is always available; it awaits the hour of our conversion" (*ibid.: PL* 133, 563). And he exclaims: "O ineffable bowels of divine piety! God pursues wrongs and yet protects sinners" (*ibid.: PL* 133, 592). Sustained by this conviction, the Abbot of Cluny used to like to pause to contemplate the mercy of Christ, the Savior whom he describes evocatively as "a lover of men": "*amator hominum Christus*" (*ibid.*, LIII: *PL* 133, 637). He observes, "Jesus took upon himself the scourging that would have been our due in order to save the creature he formed and loves" (cf. *ibid.: PL* 133, 638).

Here, a trait of the holy Abbot appears that at first sight is almost hidden beneath the rigor of his austerity as a reformer: his deep, heartfelt kindness. He was austere, but above all he was good, a man of great goodness, a goodness that comes from contact with the divine goodness. Thus Odo, his peers tell us, spread around him his overflowing joy. His biographer testifies that he never heard "such mellifluous words" on human lips (*ibid.*, I, 17: *PL* 133, 31). His biographer also records that he was in the habit of asking the children he met along the way to sing and that he would then give them some small token, and he adds: "Abbot Odo's words were full of joy ... his merriment instilled in our hearts deep joy" (*ibid.*, II, 5: *PL* 133, 63). In this way the energetic yet at the same time lovable medieval Abbot, enthusiastic about reform, with incisive action nourished in his monks, as well as in the lay faithful of his time, the resolution to progress swiftly on the path of Christian perfection.

Let us hope that his goodness, the joy that comes from faith, together with austerity and opposition to the world's vices, may also move our hearts, so that we too may find the source of the joy that flows from God's goodness.

22

Saint Peter Damian

WEDNESDAY, 9 SEPTEMBER 2009
Paul VI Audience Hall

Dear Brothers and Sisters,

During the Catecheses of these Wednesdays I am commenting on several important people in the life of the Church from her origins. Today I would like to reflect on one of the most significant figures of the eleventh century, Saint Peter Damian, a monk, a lover of solitude, and at the same time a fearless man of the Church, committed personally to the task of reform initiated by the Popes of the time. He was born in Ravenna in 1007, into a noble family but in straitened circumstances. He was left an orphan, and his childhood was not exempt from hardships and suffering, although his sister Roselinda tried to be a mother to him and his elder brother, Damian, adopted him as his son. For this very reason he was to be called Piero di Damiano, Pier Damiani [Peter of Damian, Peter Damian]. He was educated first at Faenza and then at Parma, where, already at the age of twenty-five, we find him involved in teaching. As well as a good grounding in the field of law, he acquired a refined expertise in the art of writing—the *ars scribendi*—and, thanks to his knowledge of the great Latin classics, became "one of the most accomplished Latinists of his time,

135

one of the greatest writers of medieval Latin" (J. Leclercq, *Pierre Damien, ermite et homme d'Église*, Rome, 1960, p. 172).

He distinguished himself in the widest range of literary forms: from letters to sermons, from hagiographies to prayers, from poems to epigrams. His sensitivity to beauty led him to poetic contemplation of the world. Peter Damian conceived of the universe as a never-ending "parable" and a sequence of symbols on which to base the interpretation of inner life and divine and supra-natural reality. In this perspective, in about the year 1034, contemplation of the absolute of God impelled him gradually to detach himself from the world and from its transient realities and to withdraw to the Monastery of Fonte Avellana. It had been founded only a few decades earlier but was already celebrated for its austerity. For the monks' edification he wrote the *Life* of the Founder, Saint Romuald of Ravenna, and at the same time strove to deepen their spirituality, expounding on his ideal of eremitic monasticism.

One detail should be immediately emphasized: the Hermitage at Fonte Avellana was dedicated to the Holy Cross, and the Cross was the Christian mystery that was to fascinate Peter Damian more than all the others. "Those who do not love the Cross of Christ do not love Christ", he said (*Sermo XVIII*, 11, p. 117); and he described himself as "*Petrus crucis Christi servorum famulus*: Peter, servant of the servants of the Cross of Christ" (*Ep.* 9, 1). Peter Damian addressed the most beautiful prayers to the Cross, in which he reveals a vision of this mystery which has cosmic dimensions, for it embraces the entire history of salvation: "O Blessed Cross", he exclaimed, "You are venerated, preached, and honored by the faith of the Patriarchs, the predictions of the Prophets, the senate of Apostles that judges, the victorious army of Martyrs, and the throngs of all the Saints"

(*Sermo XLVII*, 14, p. 304). Dear brothers and sisters, may the example of Saint Peter Damian spur us, too, always to look to the Cross as to the supreme act of love for humankind by God, who has given us salvation.

This great monk compiled a Rule for eremitical life in which he heavily stressed the "rigor of the hermit": in the silence of the cloister the monk is called to spend a life of prayer, by day and by night, with prolonged and strict fasting; he must put into practice generous brotherly charity in ever prompt and willing obedience to the Prior. In study and in the daily meditation of Sacred Scripture, Peter Damian discovered the mystical meaning of the Word of God, finding in it nourishment for his spiritual life. In this regard he described the hermit's cell as the "parlor in which God converses with men". For him, living as a hermit was the peak of Christian existence, "the loftiest of the states of life", because the monk, now free from the bonds of worldly life and of his own self, receives "a dowry from the Holy Spirit and his happy soul is united with its heavenly Spouse" (*Ep.* 18, 17; cf. *Ep.* 28, 43 ff.). This is important for us today, too, even though we are not monks: to know how to make silence within us to listen to God's voice, to seek, as it were, a "parlor" in which God speaks with us: learning the Word of God in prayer and in meditation is the path to life.

Saint Peter Damian, who was essentially a man of prayer, meditation, and contemplation, was also a fine theologian: his reflection on various doctrinal themes led him to important conclusions for life. Thus, for example, he expresses with clarity and liveliness the Trinitarian doctrine, already using, under the guidance of biblical and patristic texts, the three fundamental terms which were subsequently to become crucial also for the philosophy of the West: *processio*, *relatio*, and *persona* (cf. *Opusc. XXXVIII: PL* 145, 633–642; and *Opusc.*

II and III: *ibid.*, 41 ff. and 58 ff.). However, because theological analysis of the mystery led him to contemplate the intimate life of God and the dialogue of ineffable love between the three divine Persons, he drew ascetic conclusions from them for community life and even for relations between Latin and Greek Christians, divided on this topic. His meditation on the figure of Christ also had significant practical effects, since the whole of Scripture is centered on him. The "Jews", Saint Peter Damian notes, "through the pages of Sacred Scripture, bore Christ on their shoulders, as it were" (*Sermo XLVI*, 15). Therefore Christ, he adds, must be the center of the monk's life: "May Christ be heard in our language, may Christ be seen in our life, may he be perceived in our hearts" (*Sermo VIII*, 5). Intimate union with Christ engages not only monks but all the baptized. Here we find a strong appeal for us, too, not to let ourselves be totally absorbed by the activities, problems, and preoccupations of every day, forgetting that Jesus must truly be the center of our life.

Communion with Christ creates among Christians a unity of love. In Letter 28, which is a brilliant ecclesiological treatise, Peter Damian develops a profound theology of the Church as communion. "Christ's Church", he writes, is united by the bond of charity to the point that just as she has many members so is she, mystically, entirely contained in a single member; in such a way that the whole universal Church is rightly called the one Bride of Christ in the singular, and each chosen soul, through the sacramental mystery, is considered fully Church." This is important: not only that the whole universal Church should be united, but that the Church should be present in her totality in each one of us. Thus the service of the individual becomes "an expression of universality" (*Ep.* 28, 9–23). However, the ideal image of "Holy Church" illustrated by Peter Damian does not correspond—as he knew well—to the reality of his time. For this reason he did not fear to denounce the state of corruption that existed in the monasteries and among the clergy, because, above all, of the practice of the conferral by the lay authorities of ecclesiastical offices; various Bishops and Abbots were behaving as the rulers of their subjects rather than as pastors of souls. Their moral life frequently left much to be desired. For this reason, in 1057 Peter Damian left his monastery with great reluctance and sorrow and accepted, if unwillingly, his appointment as Cardinal Bishop of Ostia. So it was that he entered fully into collaboration with the Popes in the difficult task of Church reform. He had seen that contemplation was not enough and had to forgo the beauty of contemplation in order to provide his own help in the work of the Church's renewal. He thus relinquished the beauty of the hermitage and courageously undertook numerous journeys and missions.

Because of his love for monastic life, ten years later, in 1067, he obtained permission to return to Fonte Avellana and resigned from the Diocese of Ostia. However, the tranquility he had longed for did not last long: two years later, he was sent to Frankfurt in an endeavor to prevent the divorce of Henry IV from his wife, Bertha. And again, two years later, in 1071, he went to Monte Cassino for the consecration of the abbey church and, at the beginning of 1072, to Ravenna, to re-establish peace with the local Archbishop, who had supported the antipope, bringing interdiction upon the city. On the journey home to his hermitage, an unexpected illness obliged him to stop at the Benedictine Monastery of Santa Maria Vecchia Fuori Porta in Faenza, where he died in the night between 22 and 23 February 1072.

Dear brothers and sisters, it is a great grace that the Lord should have raised up in the life of the Church a figure as exuberant, rich, and complex as Saint Peter Damian. Moreover, it is rare to find theological works and spirituality as keen and vibrant as those of the Hermitage at Fonte Avellana. Saint Peter Damian was a monk through and through, with forms of austerity which to us today might even seem excessive. Yet, in that way he made monastic life an eloquent testimony of God's primacy and an appeal to all to walk toward holiness, free from any compromise with evil. He spent himself, with lucid consistency and great severity, for the reform of the Church of his time. He gave all his spiritual and physical energies to Christ and to the Church, but always remained, as he liked to describe himself, *Petrus ultimus monachorum servus*, Peter, the lowliest servant of the monks.

23

Symeon the New Theologian

WEDNESDAY, 16 SEPTEMBER 2009
Paul VI Audience Hall

Dear Brothers and Sisters,

Today we pause to reflect on an Eastern monk, Symeon
the New Theologian, whose writings have had a notable
influence on the theology and spirituality of the East, in
particular with regard to the experience of mystical union
with God. Symeon the New Theologian was born in 949
in Galatai, Paphlagonia, in Asia Minor, into a provincial
noble family. While he was still young, he moved to Constantinople to complete his education and enter the Emperor's
service. However, he did not feel attracted by the civil career
that awaited him. Under the influence of the inner illumi-
nation he was experiencing, he set out in search of some-
one who would guide him in the period of doubt and
perplexity through which he was living and help him advance
on the path of union with God. He found this spiritual
guide in Symeon the Pious (*Eulabes*), a simple monk of the
Studios in Constantinople, who advised him to read Mark
the Monk's treatise *The Spiritual Law*. Symeon the New
Theologian found in this text a teaching that made a deep
impression on him: "If you seek spiritual healing, be attentive to your conscience", he read in it. "Do all that it tells

you, and you will find what serves you." From that very moment, he himself says, he never went to sleep without first asking himself whether his conscience had anything with which to reproach him.

Symeon entered the Studite monastery, where, however, his mystical experiences and extraordinary devotion to his spiritual father caused him some difficulty. He moved to the small convent of *Saint Mamas*, also in Constantinople, of which three years later he became Abbot, *hegumen*. There he embarked on an intense quest for spiritual union with Christ which gave him great authority. It is interesting to note that he was given the title of the "New Theologian", in spite of the tradition that reserved the title of "Theologian" for two figures, John the Evangelist and Gregory Nazianzen. Symeon suffered misunderstandings and exile but was rehabilitated by Patriarch Sergius II of Constantinople.

Symeon the New Theologian spent the last stage of his life at the Monastery of Saint Marina, where he wrote a large part of his opus, becoming ever more famous for his teaching and his miracles. He died on 12 March 1022.

The best known of his disciples, Niceta Stethatos, who collected and copied Symeon's writings, compiled a post-humous edition of them and subsequently wrote his biography. Symeon's opus consists of nine volumes that are divided into *theological, gnostic, and practical chapters*, three books of *catecheses addressed to monks*, two books of *theological and ethical treatises*, and one of *hymns*. Moreover, his numerous *Letters* should not be forgotten. All these works have had an important place in the Eastern monastic tradition to our day.

Symeon focused his reflection on the Holy Spirit's presence in the baptized and on the awareness they must have of this spiritual reality. "Christian life", he emphasized, "is intimate, personal communion with God; divine grace illumines the believer's heart and leads him to a mystical vision of the Lord." Along these lines, Symeon the New Theologian insisted that true knowledge of God comes, not from books, but rather from spiritual experience, from spiritual life. Knowledge of God is born from a process of inner purification that begins with conversion of heart through the power of faith and love. It passes through profound repentance and sincere sorrow for one's sins to attain union with Christ, the source of joy and peace, suffused with the light of his presence within us. For Symeon this experience of divine grace did not constitute an exceptional gift for a few mystics but rather was the fruit of Baptism in the life of every seriously committed believer.

A point on which to reflect, dear brothers and sisters! This holy Eastern monk calls us all to pay attention to our spiritual life, to the hidden presence of God within us, to the sincerity of the conscience and to purification, to conversion of heart, so that the Holy Spirit may really become present in us and guide us. Indeed, if we are rightly concerned to care for our physical, human, and intellectual development, it is even more important not to neglect our inner growth, which consists in the knowledge of God, in true knowledge, learned not only from books but from within and in communion with God, to experience his help at every moment and in every circumstance. Basically it is this that Symeon describes when he recounts his own mystical experience. Already as a young man, before entering the monastery, while at home one night immersed in prayer and invoking God's help to fight temptations, he saw the room fill with light. Later, when he entered the monastery, he was given spiritual books for instruction, but reading them did not procure for him the peace that he sought. He felt, he himself says, as if he were a poor little bird without

wings. He humbly accepted this situation without rebel-
ling, and it was then that his visions of light began once
again to increase. Wishing to assure himself of their authenticity, Symeon asked Christ directly: "Lord, is it truly you
who are here?" He heard the affirmative answer resonating
in his heart and was supremely comforted. "That, Lord,"
he was to write later, "was the first time that you considered me, a prodigal son, worthy of hearing your voice."
However, not even this revelation left him entirely at peace.
He wondered, rather, whether he ought to consider that
experience an illusion. At last, one day an event occurred
that was crucial to his mystical experience. He began to
feel like "a poor man who loves his brethren" (*ptochós philá-
delphos*). Around him he saw hordes of enemies bent on
ensnaring him and doing him harm, yet he felt within an
intense surge of love for them. How can this be explained?
Obviously, such great love could not come from within him
but must well up from another source. Symeon realized that
it was coming from Christ present within him, and everything became clear: he had a sure proof that the source of
love in him was Christ's presence. He was certain that having in ourselves a love that exceeds our personal intentions
suggests that the source of love is in us. Thus we can say,
on the one hand, that if we are without a certain openness
to love, Christ does not enter us and, on the other, that
Christ becomes a source of love and transforms us. Dear
friends, this experience remains particularly important for
us today if we are to find the criteria that tell us whether
we are truly close to God, whether God exists and dwells
in us. God's love develops in us if we stay united to him
with prayer and with listening to his word, with an open
heart. Divine love alone prompts us to open our hearts to
others and makes us sensitive to their needs, bringing us to

consider everyone as brothers and sisters and inviting us to respond to hatred with love and to offense with forgiveness.

In thinking about this figure of Symeon the New Theologian, we may note a further element of his spirituality. On the path of ascetic life which he proposed and took, the monk's intense attention and concentration on the inner experience conferred an essential importance on the spiritual father of the monastery. The same young Symeon, as has been said, had found a spiritual director who gave him substantial help and whom he continued to hold in the greatest esteem, so great as to profess veneration for him, even in public, after his death. And I would like to say that the invitation to have recourse to a good spiritual father who can guide every individual to profound knowledge of himself and lead him to union with the Lord so that his life may be in ever closer conformity with the Gospel still applies for all priests, consecrated, and lay people, and especially youth. To go toward the Lord we always need a guide, a dialogue. We cannot do it with our thoughts alone. And this is also the meaning of the ecclesiality of our faith, of finding this guide.

To conclude, we may sum up the teaching and mystical experience of Symeon the New Theologian in these words: in his ceaseless quest for God, even amidst the difficulties he encountered and the criticism of which he was the object, in the end he let himself be guided by love. He himself was able to live and teach his monks that for every disciple of Jesus the essential thing is to grow in love; thus we grow in the knowledge of Christ himself, so as to be able to say with Saint Paul: "It is no longer I who live, but Christ who lives in me" (Gal 2:20).

24

Saint Anselm

Dear Brothers and Sisters,

The Benedictine Abbey of Sant'Anselmo [Saint Anselm] is located on the Aventine Hill in Rome. As the headquarters of an academic institute of higher studies and of the Abbot Primate of the Confederated Benedictines, it is a place that unites within it prayer, study, and governance, the same three activities that were a feature of the life of the Saint to whom it is dedicated: Anselm of Aosta, the nine hundredth anniversary of whose death occurs this year. The many initiatives promoted for this happy event, especially by the Diocese of Aosta, have highlighted the interest that this medieval thinker continues to rouse. He is also known as Anselm of Bec and Anselm of Canterbury because of the cities with which he was associated. Who is this figure to whom three places, distant from one another and located in three different nations—Italy, France, England—feel particularly bound? A monk with an intense spiritual life, an excellent teacher of the young, a theologian with an extraordinary capacity for speculation, a wise man of governance, and an intransigent defender of *libertas Ecclesiae*, of the Church's freedom, Anselm is one of the eminent figures of the Middle

Ages, who was able to harmonize all these qualities, thanks to the profound mystical experience that always guided his thought and his action.

Saint Anselm was born in 1033 (or at the beginning of 1034) in Aosta, the first child of a noble family. His father was a coarse man dedicated to the pleasures of life who squandered his possessions. On the other hand, Anselm's mother was a profoundly religious woman of high moral standing (cf. Eadmer, *Vita Sancti Anselmi*: *PL* 159, col. 49). It was she, his mother, who saw to the first human and religious formation of her son, whom she subsequently entrusted to the Benedictines at a priory in Aosta. Anselm, who since childhood—as his biographer recounts—imagined that the good Lord dwelled among the towering, snow-capped peaks of the Alps, dreamed one night that he had been invited to this splendid kingdom by God himself, who had a long and affable conversation with him and then gave him to eat "a very white bread roll" (*ibid.*, col. 51). This dream left him with the conviction that he was called to carry out a lofty mission. At the age of fifteen, he asked to be admitted to the Benedictine Order, but his father brought the full force of his authority to bear against him and did not even give way when his son, seriously ill and feeling close to death, begged for the religious habit as a supreme comfort. After his recovery and the premature death of his mother, Anselm went through a period of moral dissipation. He neglected his studies and, consumed by earthly passions, grew deaf to God's call. He left home and began to wander through France in search of new experiences. Three years later, having arrived in Normandy, he went to the Benedictine Abbey of Bec, attracted by the fame of Lanfranc of Pavia, the Prior. For him this was a providential meeting, crucial to the rest of his life. Under Lanfranc's guidance, Anselm energetically resumed his studies, and it was not long before he became not only the favorite pupil but also the confidant of the teacher. His monastic vocation was rekindled and, after careful consideration, at the age of twenty-seven he entered the monastic order and was ordained a priest. Ascesis and study unfolded new horizons before him, enabling him to rediscover at a far higher level the same familiarity with God which he had had as a child.

When Lanfranc became Abbot of Caen in 1063, Anselm, after barely three years of monastic life, was named Prior of the Monastery of Bec and teacher of the cloister school, showing his gifts as an excellent educator. He was not keen on authoritarian methods; he compared young people to small plants that develop better if they are not enclosed in greenhouses and granted them a "healthy" freedom. He was very demanding with himself and with others in monastic observance, but rather than imposing his discipline he strove to have it followed by persuasion. Upon the death of Abbot Herluin, the founder of the Abbey of Bec, Anselm was unanimously elected to succeed him; it was February 1079. In the meantime numerous monks had been summoned to Canterbury to bring to their brethren on the other side of the Channel the renewal that was being brought about on the Continent. Their work was so well received that Lanfranc of Pavia, Abbot of Caen, became the new Archbishop of Canterbury. He asked Anselm to spend a certain period with him in order to instruct the monks and to help him in the difficult plight in which his ecclesiastical community had been left after the Norman conquest. Anselm's stay turned out to be very fruitful; he won such popularity and esteem that when Lanfranc died he was chosen to succeed him in the archiepiscopal See of Canterbury. He received his solemn episcopal consecration in December 1093.

Anselm immediately became involved in a strenuous struggle for the Church's freedom, valiantly supporting the independence of the spiritual power from the temporal. Anselm defended the Church from undue interference by political authorities, especially King William Rufus and Henry I, finding encouragement and support in the Roman Pontiff, to whom he always showed courageous and cordial adherence. In 1103, this fidelity even cost him the bitterness of exile from his See of Canterbury. Moreover, it was only in 1106, when King Henry I renounced his right to the conferral of ecclesiastical offices, as well as to the collection of taxes and the confiscation of Church properties, that Anselm could return to England, where he was festively welcomed by the clergy and the people. Thus the long battle he had fought with the weapons of perseverance, pride, and goodness ended happily. This holy Archbishop, who roused such deep admiration around him wherever he went, dedicated the last years of his life to the moral formation of the clergy and to intellectual research into theological topics. He died on 21 April 1109, accompanied by the words of the Gospel proclaimed in Holy Mass on that day: "You are those who have continued with me in my trials; as my Father appointed a kingdom for me, so do I appoint for you that you may eat and drink at my table in my kingdom . . ." (Lk 22:28–30). So it was that the dream of the mysterious banquet he had had as a small boy, at the very beginning of his spiritual journey, found fulfillment. Jesus, who had invited him to sit at his table, welcomed Anselm upon his death into the eternal Kingdom of the Father.

"I pray, O God, to know you, to love you, that I may rejoice in you. And if I cannot attain to full joy in this life, may I at least advance from day to day, until that joy shall come to the full" (*Proslogion*, chapter 14). This prayer enables us to understand the mystical soul of this great Saint of the Middle Ages, the founder of scholastic theology, to whom Christian tradition has given the title: "Magnificent Doctor", because he fostered an intense desire to deepen his knowledge of the divine Mysteries but in the full awareness that the quest for God is never ending, at least on this earth. The clarity and logical rigor of his thought always aimed at "raising the mind to contemplation of God" (*ibid.*, *Proemium*). He states clearly that whoever intends to study theology cannot rely on his intelligence alone but must cultivate at the same time a profound experience of faith. The theologian's activity, according to Saint Anselm, thus develops in three stages: *faith*, a gift God freely offers, to be received with humility; *experience*, which consists in incarnating God's Word in one's own daily life; and therefore true *knowledge*, which is the fruit, never of ascetic reasoning, but rather of contemplative intuition. In this regard his famous words remain more useful than ever, even today, for healthy theological research and for anyone who wishes to deepen his knowledge of the truths of faith: "I do not endeavor, O Lord, to penetrate your sublimity, for in no wise do I compare my understanding with that; but I long to understand in some degree your truth, which my heart believes and loves. For I do not seek to understand that I may believe, but I believe in order to understand. For this also I believe, that unless I believed, I should not understand" (*ibid.*, 1).

Dear brothers and sisters, may the love of the truth and the constant thirst for God that marked Saint Anselm's entire existence be an incentive to every Christian to seek tirelessly an ever more intimate union with Christ, the Way, the Truth, and the Life. In addition, may the courageous zeal that distinguished his pastoral action and occasionally brought him misunderstanding, sorrow, and even exile be an encouragement for pastors, for consecrated people, and for all the faithful to love Christ's Church, to pray, to work, and to suffer for her, without ever abandoning or betraying her. May the Virgin Mother of God, for whom Saint Anselm had a tender, filial devotion, obtain this grace for us. "Mary, it is you whom my heart yearns to love", Saint Anselm wrote, "it is you whom my tongue ardently desires to praise."

25

Peter the Venerable

WEDNESDAY, 14 OCTOBER 2009
Saint Peter's Square

Dear Brothers and Sisters,

Peter the Venerable, whom I would like to present at today's Catechesis, takes us back to the famous Abbey of Cluny, to its *decor* (decorum) and *nitor* (clarity)—to use terms that recur in the Cluny texts—a decorum and splendor that were admired especially in the beauty of the liturgy, a privileged way for reaching God. Even more than these aspects, however, Peter's personality recalls the holiness of the great Abbots of Cluny: in Cluny "there was not a single Abbot who was not a Saint", Pope Gregory VII said in 1080. These holy men include Peter the Venerable, who possessed more or less all the virtues of his predecessors, although, under him, in comparison with the new Orders such as *Cîteaux*, Cluny began to feel some symptoms of crisis. Peter is a wonderful example of an ascetic strict with himself and understanding of others. He was born in about 1094 in the French region of Auvergne; he entered the Monastery of Sauxillanges as a child and became a monk there and then Prior. In 1122 he was elected Abbot of Cluny and remained in this office until he died, on Christmas day 1156, as he had wished. "A lover of peace," his biographer Rudolph wrote, "he obtained peace in the glory of God on the day of peace" (*Vita* I, 17: *PL* 189, 28).

All who knew him praised his refined meekness, his serene equilibrium, rectitude, loyalty, reasonableness, and his special approach to mediation. "It is in my nature", he wrote, "to be particularly inclined to indulgence; I am urged to this by my habit of forgiveness. I am accustomed to toleration and forgiveness" (*Ep.* 192, in: *The Letters of Peter the Venerable*, Harvard University Press, 1967, p. 446). He said further: "With those who hate peace let us always seek to be peacemakers" (*Ep.* 100, *loc. cit.*, p. 261). And he wrote of himself: "I am not the type who is discontented with his lot, . . . whose mind is always tormented by anxiety or doubt, and who complains that everyone else is resting while they are the only ones working" (*Ep.* 182, p. 425). With a sensitive and affectionate nature, he could combine love for the Lord with tenderness to his family members, especially his mother, and to his friends. He cultivated friendship, especially with his monks, who used to confide in him, certain that they would be heard and understood. According to his biographer's testimony: "he did not look down on anyone and never turned anyone away" (*Vita* I, 3: *PL* 189, 19); "he appeared friendly to all; in his innate goodness he was open to all" (*ibid.*, I, 1: *PL* 189, 17).

We could say that this holy Abbot also sets an example to the monks and Christians of our day, marked by a frenetic pace, when episodes of intolerance, incommunicability, division, and conflict are common. His testimony invites us to be able to combine love of God with love of neighbor and not to tire of building relations of brotherhood and reconciliation. Peter the Venerable did in fact act in this way. He found himself in charge of the Monastery of Cluny in years that were far from tranquil for various reasons, both within the Abbey and outside it, and managed to be at the same time both strict and profoundly human. He used to say: "One may obtain more from a man by tolerating him than by irritating him with reproach" (*Ep.* 172, *loc. cit.*, p. 409). By virtue of his office he had to undertake frequent journeys to Italy, England, Germany, and Spain. He found it hard to be wrenched from the quiet of contemplation. He confessed: "I go from one place to the next, I hurry, I am anxious, I am tormented, dragged here and there: my mind now on my own affairs and now on those of others, not without great mental agitation" (*Ep.* 91, *loc. cit.*, p. 233). Although he was obliged to navigate between the powers and nobles who surrounded Cluny, he succeeded in preserving his habitual calm, thanks to his sense of measure, magnanimity, and realism. Among the important figures with whom he came into contact was Bernard of Clairvaux, with whom he maintained a relationship of increasing friendship, despite the differences of their temperaments and approaches. Bernard described him as: "an important man, occupied with important affairs", and held him in high esteem (*Ep.* 147, ed. *Scriptorium Claravallense*, Milan, 1986, VI/1, pp. 658–660), while Peter the Venerable described Bernard as a "lamp of the Church" (*Ep.* 164, p. 396) and a "strong and splendid pillar of the monastic order and of the whole Church" (*Ep.* 175, p. 418).

With a lively sense of Church, Peter the Venerable affirmed that the vicissitudes of the Christian people must be felt in the "depths of the heart" by those who will be numbered "among the members of Christ's Body" (*Ep.* 164, *ibid.*, p. 397). And he added: "those who do not smart from the wounds of Christ's Body are not nourished by the Spirit of Christ", wherever they may be produced (*ibid.*). In addition, he also showed care and concern for people

outside the Church, in particular Jews and Muslims: to
increase knowledge of the latter he provided for the translation of the Qur'an. A historian recently remarked on this
subject: "In the midst of the intransigence of medieval people, even the greatest among them, we admire here a sublime example of the sensitivity to which Christian charity
leads" (J. Leclercq, *Pietro il Venerabile*, Jaca Book, 1991,
p. 189). Other aspects of Christian life dear to him were
love for the Eucharist and devotion to the Virgin Mary.
On the Blessed Sacrament he has left passages that constitute "one of the masterpieces of Eucharistic literature of
all time" (*ibid.*, p. 267), and on the Mother of God he
wrote illuminating reflections, contemplating her always in
close relationship to Jesus the Redeemer and his work of
salvation. It suffices to present his inspired prayer: "Hail,
Blessed Virgin, who put execration to flight. Hail, Mother
of the Most High, Bride of the meekest Lamb. You have
defeated the serpent, you crushed its head, when the God
you bore destroyed it.... Shining Star of the East who
dispelled the shadows of the West. Dawn who precedes
the sun, day that knows no night.... Pray God who was
born of you to dissolve our sin and, after pardoning it, to
grant us his grace and his glory" (*Carmina*: PL 189,
1018–1019).

Peter the Venerable also had a predilection for literary
activity and a gift for it. He wrote down his reflections,
persuaded of the importance of using the pen as if it were
a plough, "to scatter the seed of the Word on paper" (*Ep.*
20, p. 38). Although he was not a systematic theologian, he
was a great investigator of God's mystery. His theology is
rooted in prayer, especially in liturgical prayer, and among
the mysteries of Christ he preferred the Transfiguration,
which prefigures the Resurrection. It was Peter himself who

introduced this feast at Cluny, composing a special office for it that mirrors the characteristic theological devotion of Peter and of the Cluniac Order, which was focused entirely on contemplation of the glorious Face (*gloriosa facies*) of Christ, finding in it the reasons for that ardent joy which marked his spirit and shone out in the monastery's liturgy.

Dear brothers and sisters, this holy monk is certainly a great example of monastic holiness, nourished from the sources of the Benedictine tradition. For him, the ideal of the monk consists in "adhering tenaciously to Christ" (*Ep.* 53, *loc. cit.*, p. 161), in a cloistered life distinguished by "monastic humility" (*ibid.*) and hard work (*Ep.* 77, *loc. cit.*, p. 211) as well as an atmosphere of silent contemplation and constant praise of God. The first and most important occupation of the monk, according to Peter of Cluny, is the solemn celebration of the Divine Office—"a heavenly action and the most useful of all" (*Statutes* I, 1026)—to be accompanied by reading, meditation, personal prayer, and penance observed with discretion (cf. *Ep.* 20, *loc. cit.*, p. 40). In this way the whole of life is pervaded by profound love of God and love of others, a love that is expressed in sincere openness to neighbor, in forgiveness, and in the quest for peace. We might say, to conclude, that if this life-style, combined with daily work, was the monk's ideal for Saint Benedict, it also concerns all of us and can be to a large extent the life-style of the Christian who wants to become an authentic disciple of Christ, characterized precisely by tenacious adherence to him and by humility, diligence, and the capacity for forgiveness and peace.

26

Saint Bernard of Clairvaux

WEDNESDAY, 21 OCTOBER 2009
Saint Peter's Square

Dear Brothers and Sisters,

Today I would like to talk about Saint Bernard of Clairvaux, called "the last of the Fathers" of the Church because once again in the twelfth century he renewed and brought to the fore the important theology of the Fathers. We do not know in any detail about the years of his childhood; however, we know that he was born in 1090 in Fontaines, France, into a large and fairly well-to-do family. As a very young man he devoted himself to the study of the so-called liberal arts—especially grammar, rhetoric, and dialectics—at the school of the canons of the Church of Saint-Vorles at Châtillon-sur-Seine; and the decision to enter religious life slowly matured within him. At the age of about twenty, he entered Cîteaux, a new monastic foundation that was more flexible in comparison with the ancient and venerable monasteries of the period while at the same time stricter in the practice of the evangelical counsels. A few years later, in 1115, Bernard was sent by Stephen Harding, the third Abbot of Cîteaux, to found the monastery of Clairvaux. Here the young Abbot—he was only twenty-five years old—was able to define his conception of monastic life

and set about putting it into practice. In looking at the
discipline of other monasteries, Bernard firmly recalled the
need for a sober and measured life, at table as in clothing
and monastic buildings, and recommended the support and
care of the poor. In the meantime the community of Clairvaux became ever more numerous, and its foundations
multiplied.

In those same years before 1130, Bernard started a prolific
correspondence with many people of both important and
modest social status. To the many *Epistolae* of this period
must be added numerous *Sermones*, as well as *Sententiae* and
Tractatus. Bernard's great friendship with William, Abbot of
Saint-Thierry, and with William of Champeaux, among the
most important figures of the twelfth century, also date to
this period. From 1130 on, Bernard began to concern himself with many serious matters of the Holy See and of the
Church. For this reason he was obliged to leave his monastery ever more frequently, and he sometimes also traveled
outside France. He founded several women's monasteries and
engaged in a lively correspondence with Peter the Venerable, Abbot of Cluny, of whom I spoke last Wednesday. In
his polemical writings he targeted in particular Abelard, a
great thinker who had conceived of a new approach to theology, introducing above all the dialectic and philosophical
method in the construction of theological thought. On another
front, Bernard combated the heresy of the Cathars, who
despised matter and the human body and consequently
despised the Creator. On the other hand, he felt it was his
duty to defend the Jews and condemned the ever more widespread outbursts of anti-Semitism. With regard to this aspect
of his apostolic action, several decades later Rabbi Ephraim
of Bonn addressed a vibrant tribute to Bernard. In the same
period the holy Abbot wrote his most famous works, such

as the celebrated *Sermons on the Song of Songs [In Canticum Sermones]*. In the last years of his life—he died in 1153—Bernard was obliged to curtail his journeys but did not entirely stop traveling. He made the most of this time to review definitively the whole collection of his *Letters*, *Sermons*, and *Treatises*. Worthy of mention is a quite unusual book that he completed in this same period, in 1145, when Bernardo Pignatelli, a pupil of his, was elected Pope with the name of Eugene III. On this occasion, Bernard, as his spiritual father, dedicated to his spiritual son the text *De Consideratione* [Five Books on Consideration] which contains teachings on how to be a good Pope. In this book, which is still appropriate reading for the Popes of all times, Bernard did not only suggest how to be a good Pope, but also expressed a profound vision of the mystery of the Church and of the mystery of Christ which is ultimately resolved in contemplation of the mystery of the Triune God. "The search for this God who is not yet sufficiently sought must be continued", the holy Abbot wrote, "yet it may be easier to search for him and find him in prayer rather than in discussion. So let us end the book here, but not the search" (XIV, 32: *PL* 182, 808) and journey on toward God.

I would now like to reflect on only two of the main aspects of Bernard's rich doctrine: they concern Jesus Christ and Mary Most Holy, his Mother. His concern for the Christian's intimate and vital participation in God's love in Jesus Christ brings no new guidelines to the scientific status of theology. However, in a more decisive manner than ever, the Abbot of Clairvaux embodies the theologian, the contemplative, and the mystic. Jesus alone—Bernard insists in the face of the complex dialectical reasoning of his time—Jesus alone is "honey in the mouth, song to the ear, jubilation in the heart (*mel in ore, in aure melos, in corde iubilum*)".

The title *Doctor Mellifluus*, attributed to Bernard by tradition, stems precisely from this; indeed, his praise of Jesus Christ "flowed like honey". In the exhausting battles between Nominalists and Realists—two philosophical currents of the time—the Abbot of Clairvaux never tired of repeating that only one name counts, that of Jesus of Nazareth. "All food of the soul is dry", he professed, "unless it is moistened with this oil; insipid, unless it is seasoned with this salt. What you write has no savor for me unless I have read *Jesus* in it" (*In Canticum Sermones* XV, 6: *PL* 183, 847). For Bernard, in fact, true knowledge of God consisted in a personal, profound experience of Jesus Christ and of his love. And, dear brothers and sisters, this is true for every Christian: faith is first and foremost a personal, intimate encounter with Jesus; it is having an experience of his closeness, his friendship, and his love. It is in this way that we learn to know him ever better, to love him, and to follow him more and more. May this happen to each one of us!

In another famous *Sermon on the Sunday in the Octave of the Assumption*, the holy Abbot described with passionate words Mary's intimate participation in the redeeming sacrifice of her Son. "O Blessed Mother," he exclaimed, "a sword has truly pierced your soul! ... So deeply has the violence of pain pierced your soul that we may rightly call you more than a martyr, for in you participation in the Passion of the Son by far surpasses in intensity the physical sufferings of martyrdom" (14: *PL* 183, 437–438). Bernard had no doubts: "*per Mariam ad Iesum*", through Mary we are led to Jesus. He testifies clearly to Mary's subordination to Jesus, in accordance with the foundation of traditional Mariology. Yet the text of the *Sermon* also documents the Virgin's privileged place in the economy of salvation, subsequent to the Mother's most particular participation (*compassio*) in the sacrifice of the Son. It is not for nothing that a century and a half after Bernard's death, Dante Alighieri, in the last canticle of the *Divine Comedy*, was to put on the lips of the *Doctor Mellifluus* the sublime prayer to Mary: "Virgin Mother, daughter of your own Son, / humble and exalted more than any creature, / fixed term of the eternal counsel" (*Paradise* XXXIII, vv. 1 ff.).

These reflections, characteristic of a person in love with Jesus and Mary as was Bernard, are still a salutary stimulus not only to theologians but to all believers. Some claim to have solved the fundamental questions on God, on man, and on the world with the power of reason alone. Saint Bernard, on the other hand, solidly grounded on the Bible and on the Fathers of the Church, reminds us that without a profound faith in God, nourished by prayer and contemplation, by an intimate relationship with the Lord, our reflections on the divine mysteries risk becoming an empty intellectual exercise and losing their credibility. Theology refers us back to the "knowledge of the Saints", to their intuition of the mysteries of the living God, and to their wisdom, a gift of the Holy Spirit, which become a reference point for theological thought. Together with Bernard of Clairvaux, we too must recognize that man seeks God better and finds him more easily "in prayer than in discussion". In the end, the truest figure of a theologian and of every evangelizer remains the Apostle John, who laid his head on the Teacher's breast.

I would like to conclude these reflections on Saint Bernard with the invocations to Mary that we read in one of his beautiful homilies. "In danger, in distress, in uncertainty", he says, "think of Mary, call upon Mary. She never leaves your lips, she never departs from your heart; and so that you may obtain the help of her prayers, never forget the example of her life. If you follow her, you cannot falter; if you pray to her, you cannot despair; if you think of her, you cannot err. If she sustains you, you will not stumble; if she protects you, you have nothing to fear; if she guides you, you will never flag; if she is favorable to you, you will attain your goal ..." (*Hom. II super Missus est*, 17: *PL* 183, 70–71).

27

Monastic Theology and Scholastic Theology

WEDNESDAY, 28 OCTOBER 2009
Saint Peter's Square

Dear Brothers and Sisters,

Today I am reflecting on an interesting page of history that concerns the flourishing of Latin theology in the twelfth century, which occurred through a series of providential coincidences. A relative peace prevailed in the countries of Western Europe at that time, which guaranteed economic development and the consolidation of political structures in society, encouraging lively cultural activity also through its contacts with the East. The benefits of the vast action known as the "Gregorian reform" were already being felt within the Church. Vigorously promoted in the previous century, they had brought greater evangelical purity to the life of the ecclesial community, especially to the clergy, and had restored to the Church and to the Papacy authentic freedom of action. Furthermore, a wide-scale spiritual renewal supported by the vigorous development of consecrated life was spreading; new religious orders were coming into being and expanding, while those already in existence were experiencing a promising spiritual revival.

Theology also flourished anew, acquiring a greater awareness of its own nature: it refined its method; it tackled the new problems; advanced in the contemplation of God's mysteries; produced fundamental works; inspired important initiatives of culture, from art to literature; and prepared the masterpieces of the century to come, the century of Thomas Aquinas and Bonaventure of Bagnoregio. This intense theological activity took place in two milieus: the monasteries and the urban Schools, the *scholae*, some of which were the forerunners of universities, one of the characteristic "inventions" of the Christian Middle Ages. It is on the basis of these two milieus, monasteries and *scholae*, that it is possible to speak of the two different theological models: "monastic theology" and "Scholastic theology". The representatives of monastic theology were monks, usually Abbots, endowed with wisdom and evangelical zeal, dedicated essentially to inspiring and nourishing God's loving design. The representatives of Scholastic theology were cultured men, passionate about research; they were *magistri* anxious to show the reasonableness and soundness of the mysteries of God and of man, believed with faith, of course, but also understood by reason. Their different finalities explain the differences in their method and in their way of doing theology.

In twelfth-century monasteries the theological method mainly entailed the explanation of Sacred Scripture, the *sacra pagina*, to borrow the words of the authors of that period; biblical theology in particular was practiced. The monks, in other words, were devout listeners to and readers of the Sacred Scriptures, and one of their chief occupations consisted in *lectio divina*, that is, the prayed reading of the Bible. For them the mere reading of the Sacred Text did not suffice to perceive its profound meaning, its inner unity and transcendent message. It was therefore necessary to practice a biblical theology, in docility to the Holy Spirit. Thus, at the school of the Fathers, the Bible was interpreted allegorically in order to discover on every page of both the Old and New Testaments what it says about Christ and his work of salvation.

Last year, the Synod of Bishops on the "Word of God in the life and mission of the Church" reminded us of the importance of the spiritual approach to the Sacred Scriptures. It is useful for this purpose to take into account monastic theology, an uninterrupted biblical exegesis, as well as the works written by its exponents, precious ascetic commentaries on the Books of the Bible. Thus monastic theology incorporated the spiritual aspect into literary formation. It was aware, in other words, that a purely theoretical and secular interpretation is not enough: to enter into the heart of Sacred Scripture it must be read in the spirit in which it was written and created. Literary knowledge was necessary in order to understand the exact meaning of the words and to grasp the meaning of the text, refining the grammatical and philological sensibility. Thus *Jean Leclercq*, a Benedictine scholar in the past century, entitled the essay in which he presents the characteristics of monastic theology: *L'amour des lettres et le désir de Dieu* (Love of words and the desire for God). In fact, the desire to know and to love God which comes to meet us through his words, which are to be received, meditated upon, and put into practice, leads us to seek to deepen our knowledge of the biblical texts in all their dimensions. Then there is another attitude on which those who practice monastic theology insist: namely, an intimate, prayerful disposition that must precede, accompany, and complete the study of Sacred Scripture. Since, ultimately, monastic theology is listening to God's Word, the heart must be purified in order to receive it, and, especially, a longing must be enkindled in it to encounter the Lord. Theology thus becomes meditation, prayer, a song of praise, and impels us to sincere conversion. On this path, many exponents of monastic theology attained the highest goals of mystic experience and extend an invitation to us, too, to nourish our lives with the Word of God, for example, through listening more attentively to the Readings and the Gospel, especially during Sunday Mass. It is also important to set aside a certain period each day for meditation on the Bible, so that the Word of God may be a light that illumines our daily pilgrimage on earth.

Scholastic theology, on the other hand—as I was saying—was practiced at the *scholae* which came into being beside the great cathedrals of that time for the formation of the clergy or around a teacher of theology and his disciples to train professionals of culture in a period in which the appreciation of knowledge was constantly growing. Central to the method of the Scholastics was the *quaestio*, that is, the problem the reader faces in approaching the words of Scripture and of tradition. In the face of the problem that these authoritative texts pose, questions arise and the debate between teacher and student comes into being. In this discussion, on the one hand, the arguments of the authority appear and, on the other, those of reason, and the ensuing discussion seeks to come to a synthesis between authority and reason in order to reach a deeper understanding of the Word of God. In this regard, Saint Bonaventure said that theology is *"per additionem"* (cf. *Commentaria in quatuor libros sententiarum* I, *proem.*, q. 1, *concl.*), that is, theology adds the dimension of reason to the Word of God and thus creates a faith that is deeper, more personal, hence also more concrete in the person's life. In this regard, various solutions were found and conclusions reached which began to build a system of theology. The organization of the *quaestiones* led to the compilation of ever more extensive syntheses, that is, the different *quaestiones* were composed with the answers elicited, thereby creating a synthesis, the *summae*, which were in reality extensive theological and dogmatic treatises born from the confrontation of human reason with the Word of God. Scholastic theology aimed to present the unity and harmony of the Christian Revelation with a method, called, precisely "Scholastic", of the school, which places trust in human reason. Grammar and philology are at the service of theological knowledge, but logic even more so, namely, the discipline that studies the "functioning" of human reasoning, in such a way that the truth of a proposal appears obvious. Still today, in reading the Scholastic *summae* one is struck by the order, clarity, and logical continuity of the arguments and by the depth of certain insights. With technical language a precise meaning is attributed to every word, and, between believing and understanding, a reciprocal movement of clarification is established.

Dear brothers and sisters, in echoing the invitation of the First Letter of Peter, Scholastic theology stimulates us to be ever ready to account for the hope that is in us (cf. 3:15), hearing the questions as our own and thus also being capable of giving an answer. It reminds us that a natural friendship exists between faith and reason, founded in the order of Creation itself. In the *incipit* of the Encyclical *Fides et Ratio*, the Servant of God John Paul II wrote: "Faith and reason are like two wings on which the human spirit rises to the contemplation of truth." Faith is open to the effort of understanding by reason; reason, in turn, recognizes that faith does not demean her but on the contrary impels her toward vaster and loftier horizons. The eternal lesson of monastic theology fits in here. Faith and reason, in reciprocal dialogue, are vibrant with joy when they are both inspired by the search for intimate union with God. When love enlivens the prayerful dimension of theology, knowledge, acquired by reason, is broadened. Truth is sought with humility, received with wonder and gratitude: in a word, knowledge only grows if one loves truth. Love becomes intelligence and authentic theology wisdom of the heart, which directs and sustains the faith and life of believers. Let us therefore pray that the journey of knowledge and of the deepening of God's mysteries may always be illumined by divine love.

28

Two Theological Models in Comparison: Bernard and Abelard

WEDNESDAY, 4 NOVEMBER 2009
Saint Peter's Square

Dear Brothers and Sisters,

In my last Catechesis I presented the main features of twelfth-century monastic theology, and Scholastic theology, which, in a certain sense, we might call respectively "theology of the heart" and "theology of reason". Among the exponents of both these theological currents a broad and at times heated discussion developed, symbolically represented by the controversy between Saint Bernard of Clairvaux and Abelard.

In order to understand this confrontation between the two great teachers, it helps to remember that theology is the search for a rational understanding, as far as this is possible, of the mysteries of Christian Revelation, believed through faith: *fides quaerens intellectum*—faith seeking understanding—to borrow a traditional, concise, and effective definition. Now, whereas Saint Bernard, a staunch representative of monastic theology, puts the accent on the first part of the definition, namely, on *fides*, faith, Abelard, who was a Scholastic, insists on the second part, that is, on the *intellectus*, on understanding through reason. For Bernard, faith itself is endowed with a deep certitude based on the testimony of Scripture and on the teaching of the Church Fathers. Faith, moreover, is reinforced by the witness of the Saints and by the inspiration of the Holy Spirit in the individual believer's soul. In cases of doubt and ambiguity, faith is protected and illumined by the exercise of the Magisterium of the Church. So it was that Bernard had difficulty in reaching agreement with Abelard and, more in general, with those who submitted the truths of faith to the critical examination of the intellect; an examination which in his opinion entailed a serious danger, that is, intellectualism, the relativization of truth, the questioning of the actual truths of faith. In this approach, Bernard saw audacity taken to the point of unscrupulousness, a product of the pride of human intelligence that claims to "grasp" the mystery of God. In a letter he writes with regret: "Human ingenuity takes possession of everything, leaving nothing to faith. It confronts what is above and beyond it, scrutinizes what is superior to it, bursts into the world of God, alters rather than illumines the mysteries of faith; it does not open what is closed and sealed but rather uproots it, and what it does not find viable in itself it considers as nothing and refuses to believe in it" (*Epistola* CLXXXVIII, 1: *PL* 182, 1, 353).

Theology for Bernard had a single purpose: to encourage the intense and profound experience of God. Theology is therefore an aid to loving the Lord ever more and ever better, as the title of his treatise *On Loving God* says (*Liber de diligendo Deo*). On this journey there are various stages that Bernard describes in detail, which lead to the crowning experience when the believer's soul becomes inebriated in ineffable love. Already on earth the human soul can attain this mystical union with the divine Word, a union that the *Doctor Mellifluus* describes as "spiritual nuptials".

The divine Word visits the soul, eliminates the last traces of resistance, illuminates, inflames, and transforms it. In this mystical union the soul enjoys great serenity and sweetness and sings a hymn of joy to its Bridegroom. As I mentioned in the Catechesis on the life and doctrine of Saint Bernard, theology for him could not but be nourished by contemplative prayer, in other words, by the affective union of the heart and the mind with God.

On the other hand, Abelard, who among other things was the very person who introduced the term "theology" in the sense in which we understand it today, puts himself in a different perspective. Born in Brittany, France, this famous teacher of the twelfth century was endowed with a keen intelligence, and his vocation was to study. He first concerned himself with philosophy and then applied the results he achieved in this discipline to theology, which he taught in Paris, the most cultured city of the time, and later in the monasteries in which he lived. He was a brilliant orator: literally crowds of students attended his lectures. He had a religious spirit but a restless personality, and his life was full of dramatic events: he contested his teachers, and he had a son by Héloïse, a cultured and intelligent woman. He often argued with his theological colleagues and also underwent ecclesiastical condemnations, although he died in full communion with the Church, submitting to her authority with a spirit of faith. Actually Saint Bernard contributed to condemning certain teachings of Abelard at the Provincial Synod of Sens in 1140 and went so far as to request Pope Innocent II's intervention. The Abbot of Clairvaux contested, as we have seen, the excessively intellectualistic method of Abelard, who in his eyes reduced faith to mere opinion, detached from the revealed truth. Bernard's fears were not unfounded and were, moreover, shared by other great thinkers of his time. Indeed, an excessive use of philosophy dangerously weakened Abelard's Trinitarian teaching, hence also his idea of God. In the moral field his teaching was not devoid of ambiguity: he insisted on considering the intention of the subject as the sole source for defining the goodness or evil of moral acts, thereby neglecting the objective significance and moral value of the actions: a dangerous subjectivism. This as we know is a very timely aspect for our epoch, in which all too often culture seems to be marked by a growing tendency to ethical relativism; the self alone decides what is good for it, for oneself, at this moment. However, the great merits of Abelard, who had many disciples and made a crucial contribution to the development of Scholastic theology destined to be expressed in a more mature and fruitful manner in the following century, should not be forgotten. Nor should some of his insights be underestimated, such as, for example, his affirmation that non-Christian religious traditions already contain a preparation for the acceptance of Christ, the divine Word.

What can we learn today from the confrontation, frequently in very heated tones, between Bernard and Abelard and, in general, between monastic theology and Scholastic theology? First of all, I believe that it demonstrates the usefulness and need for healthy theological discussion within the Church, especially when the questions under discussion are not defined by the Magisterium, which nevertheless remains an ineluctable reference point. Saint Bernard, but also Abelard himself, always recognized her authority unhesitatingly. Furthermore, Abelard's condemnation on various occasions reminds us that in the theological field there must be a balance between what we may call the architectural principles given to us by Revelation, which therefore always retain their prime importance, and the principles for interpretation suggested by philosophy, that is, by reason, which have an important but exclusively practical role. When this balance between the architecture and the instruments for interpretation is lacking, theological reflection risks being distorted by errors, and it is then the task of the Magisterium to exercise that necessary service to the truth which belongs to it. It must be emphasized in addition that among the reasons that induced Bernard to "take sides" against Abelard and to call for the intervention of the Magisterium was also his concern to safeguard simple and humble believers, who must be defended when they risk becoming confused or misled by excessively personal opinions or by anti-conformist theological argumentation that might endanger their faith.

Lastly, I would like to recall that the theological confrontation between Bernard and Abelard ended with their complete reconciliation, thanks to the mediation of a common friend, Peter the Venerable, the Abbot of Cluny of whom I have spoken in one of my previous Catecheses. Abelard showed humility in recognizing his errors, Bernard used great benevolence. They both upheld the most important value in a theological controversy: to preserve the Church's faith and to make the truth in charity triumph. Today, too, may this be the attitude with which we confront one another in the Church, having as our goal the constant quest for truth.

29

The Cluniac Reform

WEDNESDAY, 11 NOVEMBER 2009
Paul VI Audience Hall

Dear Brothers and Sisters,

This morning I would like to speak to you about a monastic movement that was very important in the Middle Ages and which I have already mentioned in previous Catecheses. It is the Order of Cluny, which at the beginning of the twelfth century, at the height of its expansion, had almost 1,200 monasteries: a truly impressive figure! A monastery was founded at Cluny in 910, precisely 1,100 years ago, and subsequent to the donation of William the Pious, Duke of Aquitaine, was placed under the guidance of Abbot Berno. At that time, Western monasticism, which had flourished several centuries earlier with Saint Benedict, was experiencing a severe decline for various reasons: unstable political and social conditions due to the continuous invasions and sacking by peoples who were not integrated into the fabric of Europe, widespread poverty, and, especially, the dependence of abbeys on the local nobles who controlled all that belonged to the territories under their jurisdiction. In this context, Cluny was the heart and soul of a profound renewal of monastic life that led it back to its original inspiration.

At Cluny, the Rule of Saint Benedict was restored with several adaptations which had already been introduced by other reformers. The main objective was to guarantee the central role that the liturgy must have in Christian life. The Cluniac monks devoted themselves with love and great care to the celebration of the Liturgical Hours, to the singing of the Psalms, to processions as devout as they were solemn, and above all, to the celebration of Holy Mass. They promoted sacred music; they wanted architecture and art to contribute to the beauty and solemnity of the rites; they enriched the liturgical calendar with special celebrations, such as, for example, at the beginning of November, the Commemoration of All Souls, which we, too, have just celebrated; and they intensified the devotion to the Virgin Mary. Great importance was given to the liturgy because the monks of Cluny were convinced that it was participation in the liturgy of Heaven. And the monks felt responsible for interceding at the altar of God for the living and the dead, given large numbers of the faithful were insistently asking them to be remembered in prayer. Moreover, it was with this same aim that William the Pious had desired the foundation of the Abbey of Cluny. In the ancient document that testifies to the foundation we read: "With this gift I establish that a monastery of regulars be built at Cluny in honor of the Holy Apostles Peter and Paul, where monks who live according to the Rule of Saint Benedict shall gather ... so that a venerable sanctuary of prayer with vows and supplications may be visited there, and the heavenly life be sought after and yearned for with every desire and with deep ardor, and that assiduous prayers, invocations, and supplications be addressed to the Lord." To preserve and foster this atmosphere of prayer, the Cluniac Rule emphasized the importance of silence, to which discipline the monks willingly submitted, convinced that the purity of the virtues to which they aspired demanded deep and constant recollection. It is not surprising that before long the Monastery of Cluny gained a reputation for holiness and that many other monastic communities decided to follow its discipline. Numerous princes and Popes asked the Abbots of Cluny to extend their reform so that in a short time a dense network of monasteries developed that were linked to Cluny, either by true and proper juridical bonds or by a sort of charismatic affiliation. Thus a spiritual Europe gradually took shape in the various regions of France and in Italy, Spain, Germany, and Hungary.

Cluny's success was assured primarily not only by the lofty spirituality cultivated there, but also by several other conditions that ensured its development. In comparison with what had happened until then, the Monastery of Cluny and the communities dependent upon it were recognized as exempt from the jurisdiction of the local Bishops and were directly subject to that of the Roman Pontiff. This meant that Cluny had a special bond with the See of Peter, and, precisely because of the protection and encouragement of the Pontiffs, the ideals of purity and fidelity proposed by the Cluniac Reform spread rapidly. Furthermore, the Abbots were elected without any interference from the civil authorities, unlike what happened in other places. Truly worthy people succeeded one another at the helm of Cluny and of the numerous monastic communities dependent upon it: Abbot Odo of Cluny, of whom I spoke in a Catechesis two months ago, and other great figures, such as Eymard, Majolus, Odilo, and especially Hugh the Great, who served for long periods, thereby assuring stability and the spread of the reform embarked upon. Not only Odo, but also Majolus, Odilo, and Hugh are venerated as Saints.

The Cluniac Reform had positive effects not only in the purification and reawakening of monastic life, but also in the life of the universal Church. In fact, the aspiration to evangelical perfection was an incentive to fight two great abuses that afflicted the Church in that period: simony, that is, the acquisition of pastoral offices for money, and immorality among the secular clergy. The Abbots of Cluny with their spiritual authority, the Cluniac monks who became Bishops and some of them even Popes, took the lead in this impressive action of spiritual renewal. And it yielded abundant fruit: celibacy was once again esteemed and practiced by priests, and more transparent procedures were introduced in the designation of ecclesiastical offices.

Also significant were the benefits that monasteries, inspired by the Cluniac Reform, contributed to society. At a time when Church institutions alone provided for the poor, charity was practiced with dedication. In all the houses, the almoner was bound to offer hospitality to needy wayfarers and pilgrims, traveling priests and religious, and especially the poor, who came asking for food and a roof over their heads for a few days. Equally important were two other institutions promoted by Cluny that were characteristic of medieval civilization: the "Truce of God" and the "Peace of God". In an epoch heavily marked by violence and the spirit of revenge, with the "Truces of God" long periods of non-belligerence were guaranteed, especially on the occasion of specific religious feasts and certain days of the week. With "the Peace of God", on pain of a canonical reprimand, respect was requested for defenseless people and for sacred places.

In this way, in the conscience of the peoples of Europe during that long process of gestation, which was to lead to their ever clearer recognition, two fundamental elements for the construction of society matured, namely, the value of the human person and the primary good of peace. Furthermore, as happened for other monastic foundations, the Cluniac monasteries had likewise at their disposal extensive properties which, diligently put to good use, helped to develop the economy. Alongside the manual work there was no lack of the typical cultural activities of medieval monasticism, such as schools for children, the foundation of libraries, and *scriptoria* for the transcription of books.

In this way, one thousand years ago, when the development of the European identity had gathered momentum, the experience of Cluny, which had spread across vast regions of the European Continent, made its important and precious contribution. It recalled the primacy of spiritual benefits; it kept alive the aspiration to the things of God; it inspired and encouraged initiatives and institutions for the promotion of human values; it taught a spirit of peace. Dear brothers and sisters, let us pray that all those who have at heart an authentic humanism and the future of Europe may be able to rediscover, appreciate, and defend the rich cultural and religious heritage of these centuries.

30

The Cathedral from the Romanesque
to the Gothic Architecture:
The Theological Background

WEDNESDAY, 18 NOVEMBER 2009
Paul VI Audience Hall

Dear Brothers and Sisters,

In the Catecheses of the past few weeks I have presented
several aspects of medieval theology. The Christian faith,
however, deeply rooted in the men and women of those
centuries, did not only give rise to masterpieces of theological literature, thought, and faith. It also inspired one of
the loftiest expressions of universal civilization: the cathedral, the true glory of the Christian Middle Ages. Indeed,
for about three centuries, from the beginning of the eleventh century, Europe experienced extraordinary artistic creativity and fervor. An ancient chronicler described the
enthusiasm and the hard-working spirit of those times in
these words: "It happens that throughout the world, but
especially in Italy and in Gaul, people began rebuilding
churches, although many had no need of such restoration
because they were still in good condition. It was like a com-
petition between one people and another; one might have
believed that the world, shaking off its rags and tatters, wanted

to be reclad throughout in the white mantle of new churches. In short, all these cathedral churches, a large number of monastic churches, and even village oratories were restored by the faithful at that time" (Rodolphus Glaber, *Historiarum, libri quinque*, 3, 4).

Various factors contributed to this rebirth of religious architecture. First of all, there were more favorable historical conditions, such as greater political stability, accompanied by a constant increase in the population and the gradual development of the cities, trade, and wealth. Furthermore, architects found increasingly complicated technical solutions to increase the size of buildings, at the same time guaranteeing them both soundness and majesty. It was mainly thanks to the enthusiasm and spiritual zeal of monasticism, at the height of its expansion, that abbey churches were built in which the liturgy might be celebrated with dignity and solemnity. They became the destination of continuous pilgrimages, where the faithful, attracted by the veneration of Saints' relics, could pause in prayer. So it was that the Romanesque churches and cathedrals came into being. They were characterized by the extended length of the aisles, in order to accommodate numerous faithful. They were very solid churches with thick walls, stone vaults, and simple, spare lines. An innovation was the introduction of sculptures. Because Romanesque churches were places for monastic prayer and for the worship of the faithful, the sculptors, rather than being concerned with technical perfection, turned their attention in particular to the educational dimension. Since it was necessary to inspire in souls strong impressions, sentiments that could persuade them to shun vice and evil and to practice virtue and goodness, the recurrent theme was the portrayal of Christ as Universal Judge surrounded by figures of the Apocalypse. It was usually the portals of the Romanesque churches which displayed these figures, to emphasize that Christ is the Door that leads to Heaven. On crossing the threshold of the sacred building, the faithful entered a space and time different from that of their ordinary life. Within the church, believers in a sovereign, just, and merciful Christ in the artists' intention could enjoy in anticipation eternal beatitude in the celebration of the liturgy and of devotional acts carried out in the sacred building.

In the twelfth and thirteenth centuries another kind of architecture for sacred buildings spread from the north of France: the Gothic. It had two new characteristics in comparison with the Romanesque, a soaring upward movement and luminosity. Gothic cathedrals show a synthesis of faith and art harmoniously expressed in the fascinating universal language of beauty which still elicits wonder today. By the introduction of vaults with pointed arches supported by robust pillars, it was possible to increase their height considerably. The upward thrust was intended as an invitation to prayer and at the same time was itself a prayer. Thus the Gothic cathedral intended to express in its architectural lines the soul's longing for God. In addition, by employing the new technical solutions, it was possible to make openings in the outer walls and to embellish them with stained-glass windows. In other words, the windows became great luminous images, very suitable for instructing the people in faith. In them, scene by scene, the life of a Saint, a parable, or some other biblical event was recounted. A cascade of light poured through the stained-glass upon the faithful to tell them the story of salvation and to involve them in this story.

Another merit of Gothic cathedrals is that the whole Christian and civil community participated in their building and decoration in harmonious and complementary ways. The lowly and the powerful, the illiterate and the learned; all participated because in this common house all believers were instructed in the faith. Gothic sculpture, in fact, has made cathedrals into "stone Bibles", depicting Gospel episodes and illustrating the content of the liturgical year, from the Nativity to the glorification of the Lord. In those centuries, too, the perception of the Lord's humanity became ever more widespread, and the sufferings of his Passion were represented realistically: the suffering Christ (*Christus patiens*) became an image beloved by all and apt to inspire devotion and repentance for sins. Nor were Old Testament figures lacking; thus to the faithful who went to the cathedral their histories became familiar as part of the one common history of salvation. With faces full of beauty, gentleness, and intelligence, Gothic sculpture of the thirteenth century reveals a happy and serene religious sense, glad to show a heartfelt filial devotion to the Mother of God, sometimes seen as a young woman, smiling and motherly, but mainly portrayed as the Queen of Heaven and earth, powerful and merciful. The faithful who thronged the Gothic cathedrals also liked to find Saints there, expressed in works of art, models of Christian life and intercessors with God. And there was no shortage of the "secular" scenes of life; thus, here and there, there are depictions of work in the fields, of the sciences and arts. All was oriented and offered to God in the place in which the liturgy was celebrated. We may understand better the meaning attributed to a Gothic cathedral by reflecting on the text of the inscription engraved on the central portal of Saint-Denis in Paris: "Passerby, who are stirred to praise the beauty of these doors, do not let yourself be dazzled by the gold or by the magnificence, but rather by the painstaking work. Here a famous work shines out, but may Heaven deign that this famous work that shines make spirits resplendent so that, with the luminous truth, they may walk toward the true light, where Christ is the true door."

Dear brothers and sisters, I would now like to emphasize two elements of Romanesque and Gothic art that are also helpful to us. The first: the masterpieces of art created in Europe in past centuries are incomprehensible unless one takes into account the religious spirit that inspired them. Marc Chagall, an artist who has always witnessed to the encounter between aesthetics and faith, wrote that "For centuries painters dipped their brushes into that colorful alphabet which was the Bible." When faith, celebrated in the liturgy in a special way, encounters art, it creates a profound harmony because each can and wishes to speak of God, making the Invisible visible. I would like to share this encounter with artists on 21 November, renewing to them the proposal of friendship between Christian spirituality and art that my venerable Predecessors hoped for, especially the Servants of God Paul VI and John Paul II. The second element: the strength of the Romanesque style and the splendor of the Gothic cathedrals remind us that the *via pulchritudinis*, the way of beauty, is a privileged and fascinating path on which to approach the mystery of God. What is the beauty that writers, poets, musicians, and artists contemplate and express in their language other than the reflection of the splendor of the eternal Word made flesh? Then Saint Augustine says:

> Question the beauty of the earth, question the beauty of the sea, question the beauty of the air, amply spread around everywhere, question the beauty of the sky, question the serried ranks of the stars, question the sun making the day glorious with its bright beams, question the moon tempering the darkness of the following night with its shining rays, question the animals that move in the waters, that amble about on dry land, that fly in the air; their souls hidden,

their bodies evident; the visible bodies needing to be controlled, the invisible souls controlling them. Question all these things. They all answer you, 'Here we are, look; we're beautiful!' Their beauty is their confession. Who made these beautiful changeable things if not one who is beautiful and unchangeable? (*Sermo* CCXLI, 2: *PL* 38, 1134)

Dear brothers and sisters, may the Lord help us to rediscover the way of beauty as one of the itineraries, perhaps the most attractive and fascinating, on which to succeed in encountering and loving God.

31

Hugh and Richard of Saint-Victor

WEDNESDAY, 25 NOVEMBER 2009
Paul VI Audience Hall

Dear Brothers and Sisters,

At these Wednesday Audiences I am presenting several exemplary figures of believers who were dedicated to showing the harmony between reason and faith and to witnessing with their lives to the proclamation of the Gospel. I intend to speak today about Hugh and Richard of Saint-Victor. Both were among those philosophers and theologians known as "Victorines" because they lived and taught at the Abbey of Saint-Victor in Paris, founded at the beginning of the twelfth century by William of Champeaux. William himself was a well-known teacher who succeeded in giving his abbey a solid cultural identity. Indeed, a school for the formation of the monks, also open to external students, was founded at Saint-Victor, where a felicitous synthesis was achieved between the two theological models of which I have spoken in previous Catecheses. These are monastic theology, primarily oriented to contemplation of the mysteries of the faith in Scripture; and Scholastic theology, which aimed to use reason to scrutinize these mysteries with innovative methods in order to create a theological system.

We have little information about the life of Hugh of Saint-Victor. The date and place of his birth are uncertain; he may have been born in Saxony or in Flanders. It is known that having arrived in Paris, the European cultural capital at that time, he spent the rest of his days at the Abbey of Saint-Victor, where he was first a disciple and subsequently a teacher. Even before his death in 1141, he earned great fame and esteem, to the point that he was called a "second Saint Augustine". Like Augustine, in fact, he meditated deeply on the relationship between faith and reason, between the secular sciences and theology. According to Hugh of Saint-Victor, in addition to being useful for understanding the Scriptures, all the branches of knowledge have intrinsic value and must be cultivated in order to broaden human knowledge as well as to answer the human longing to know the truth. This healthy intellectual curiosity led him to counsel students always to give free rein to their desire to learn. In his treatise on the methodology of knowledge and pedagogy, entitled significantly *Didascalicon* (On teaching) his recommendation was: "Learn willingly what you do not know from everyone. The person who has sought to learn something from everyone will be wiser than them all. The person who receives something from everyone ends by becoming the richest of all" (*Eruditiones Didascalicae* 3, 14: *PL* 176, 774).

The knowledge with which the philosophers and theologians known as *Victorines* were concerned in particular was theology, which requires first and foremost the loving study of Sacred Scripture. In fact, in order to know God, one cannot but begin with what God himself has chosen to reveal of himself in the Scriptures. In this regard, Hugh of Saint-Victor is a typical representative of monastic theology, based entirely on biblical exegesis. To interpret

Scripture, he suggests the traditional Patristic and medieval structure, namely, the literal and historical sense first of all, then the allegorical and anagogical, and, lastly, the moral. These are four dimensions of the meaning of Scripture that are being rediscovered even today. For this reason one sees that in the text and in the proposed narrative a more profound meaning is concealed: the thread of faith that leads us heavenward and guides us on this earth, teaching us how to live. Yet, while respecting these four dimensions of the meaning of Scripture, in an original way in comparison with his contemporaries, Hugh of Saint-Victor insists—and this is something new—on the importance of the historical and literal meaning. In other words, before discovering the symbolic value, the deeper dimensions of the biblical text, it is necessary to know and to examine the meaning of the event as it is told in Scripture. Otherwise, he warns, using an effective comparison, one risks being like grammarians who do not know the alphabet. To those who know the meaning of history as described in the Bible, human events appear marked by divine Providence, in accordance with a clearly ordained plan. Thus, for Hugh of Saint-Victor, history is neither the outcome of a blind destiny nor as meaningless as it might seem. On the contrary, the Holy Spirit is at work in human history and inspires the marvelous dialogue of human beings with God, their friend. This theological view of history highlights the astonishing and salvific intervention of God, who truly enters and acts in history. It is almost as if he takes part in our history, while ever preserving and respecting the human being's freedom and responsibility.

Our author considered that the study of Sacred Scripture and its historical and literal meaning makes possible true and proper theology, that is, the systematic illustration of truths, knowledge of their structure, the illustration of the dogmas of the faith. He presents these in a solid synthesis in his Treatise *De Sacramentis Christianae Fidei* (The sacraments of the Christian faith). Among other things, he provides a definition of "sacrament" which, further perfected by other theologians, contains ideas that are still very interesting today. "The sacrament is a corporeal or material element proposed in an external and tangible way", he writes, "which by its likeness *makes present* an invisible and spiritual grace; it *signifies* it, because it was instituted to this end, and *contains* it, because it is capable of sanctifying" (9, 2: *PL* 176, 317). On the one hand is the visibility in the symbol, the "corporeity" of the gift of God. On the other hand, however, in it is concealed the divine grace that comes from the history of Jesus Christ, who himself created the fundamental symbols. Therefore, there are three elements that contribute to the definition of a sacrament, according to Hugh of Saint-Victor: the institution by Christ; the communication of grace; and the analogy between the visible or material element and the invisible element: the divine gifts. This vision is very close to our contemporary understanding, because the sacraments are presented with a language interwoven with symbols and images capable of speaking directly to the human heart. Today, too, it is important that liturgical animators, and priests in particular, with pastoral wisdom, give due weight to the signs proper to sacramental rites—to this visibility and tangibility of grace. They should pay special attention to catechesis, to ensure that all the faithful experience every celebration of the sacraments with devotion, intensity, and spiritual joy.

Richard, who came from Scotland, was Hugh of Saint-Victor's worthy disciple. He was Prior of the Abbey of

Saint-Victor from 1162 to 1173, the year of his death. Richard, too, of course, assigned a fundamental role to the study of the Bible but, unlike his master, gave priority to the allegorical sense, the symbolic meaning of Scripture. This is what he uses, for example, in his interpretation of the Old Testament figure of Benjamin, the son of Jacob, as a model of contemplation and the epitome of the spiritual life. Richard addresses this topic in two texts, *Benjamin Minor* and *Benjamin Maior*. In these he proposes to the faithful a spiritual journey which is primarily an invitation to exercise the various virtues, learning to discipline and to control with reason the sentiments and the inner affective and emotional impulses. Only when the human being has attained balance and human maturity in this area is he or she ready to approach contemplation, which Richard defines as "a profound and pure gaze of the soul, fixed on the marvels of wisdom, combined with an ecstatic sense of wonder and admiration" (*Benjamin Maior* 1, 4: *PL* 196, 67).

Contemplation is therefore the destination, the result of an arduous journey that involves dialogue between faith and reason that is once again a theological discourse. Theology stems from truths that are the subject of faith but seeks to deepen knowledge of them by the use of reason, taking into account the gift of faith. This application of reason to the comprehension of faith is presented convincingly in Richard's masterpiece, one of the great books of history, the *De Trinitate* (The Trinity). In the six volumes of which it is composed, he reflects perspicaciously on the mystery of the Triune God. According to our author, since God is love, the one divine substance includes communication, oblation, and love between the two Persons, the Father and the Son, who are placed in a reciprocal, eternal exchange of

love. However, the perfection of happiness and goodness
admits of no exclusivism or closure. On the contrary, it
requires the eternal presence of a third Person, the Holy
Spirit. Trinitarian love is participatory and harmonious and
includes a superabundance of delight, enjoyment, and ceaseless joy. Richard, in other words, supposes that God is love,
analyzes the essence of love, of what the reality love entails,
and thereby arrives at the Trinity of the Persons, which
really is the logical expression of the fact that God is love.

Yet Richard is aware that love, although it reveals to us
the essence of God, although it makes us "understand" the
mystery of the Trinity, is nevertheless always an analogy that
serves to speak of a mystery that surpasses the human mind.
Being the poet and mystic that he is, Richard also has
recourse to other images. For example, he compares divinity to a river, to a loving wave which originates in the Father
and ebbs and flows in the Son, to be subsequently spread
with joy through the Holy Spirit.

Dear friends, authors such as Hugh and Richard of Saint-
Victor raise our minds to contemplation of the divine realities. At the same time, the immense joy we feel at the
thought, admiration, and praise of the Blessed Trinity sup-
ports and sustains the practical commitment to be inspired
by this perfect model of communion in love in order to
build our daily human relationships. The Trinity is truly
perfect communion! How the world would change if relations were always lived in families, in parishes, and in every
other community by following the example of the three
divine Persons, in whom each lives not only *with* the other,
but *for* the other and *in* the other! A few months ago at the
Angelus I recalled: "Love alone makes us happy because we
live in a relationship, and we live to love and to be loved"
(*Angelus*, Trinity Sunday, 7 June 2009). It is love that works

this ceaseless miracle. As in the life of the Blessed Trinity, plurality is recomposed in unity, where all is kindness and joy. With Saint Augustine, held in great honor by the *Victorines*, we too may exclaim: "*Vides Trinitatem, si caritatem vides*—you contemplate the Trinity if you see charity" (*De Trinitate* VIII, 8, 12).

32

William of Saint-Thierry

WEDNESDAY, 2 DECEMBER 2009
Saint Peter's Square

Dear Brothers and Sisters,

In a previous Catechesis I presented Bernard of Clairvaux, the "Doctor Mellifluus", a great protagonist of the twelfth century. His biographer, a friend who esteemed him, was William of Saint-Thierry on whom I am reflecting in this morning's Catechesis.

William was born in Liège between 1075 and 1080. From a noble family and endowed with a keen intelligence and an innate love of study, he attended famous schools of the time, such as those in his native city and in Rheims, France. He also came into personal contact with Abelard, the teacher who applied philosophy to theology in such an original way as to give rise to great perplexity and opposition. William also expressed his own reservations, pressing his friend Bernard to take a stance concerning Abelard. Responding to God's mysterious and irresistible call which is the vocation to the consecrated life, William entered the Benedictine Monastery of Saint-Nicasius in Rheims in 1113. A few years later he became Abbot of the Monastery of Saint-Thierry in the Diocese of Rheims. In that period, there was a widespread need for the purification and renewal of monastic life to make it authentically evangelical. William worked on doing this in his own monastery and in general in the Benedictine Order. However, he met with great resistance to his attempts at reform, and thus, although his friend Bernard advised him against it, in 1135 he left the Benedictine abbey and exchanged his black habit for a white one in order to join the Cistercians of Signy. From that time, until his death in 1148, he devoted himself to prayerful contemplation of God's mysteries, ever the subject of his deepest desires, and to the composition of spiritual literature, important writings in the history of monastic theology.

One of his first works is entitled *De Natura et dignitate amoris* (The nature and dignity of love). In it William expressed one of his basic ideas that is also valid for us. The principal energy that moves the human soul, he said, is love. Human nature, in its deepest essence, consists in loving. Ultimately, a single task is entrusted to every human being: to learn to like and to love, sincerely, authentically, and freely. However, it is only from God's teaching that this task is learned and that the human being may reach the end for which he was created. Indeed, William wrote: "The art of arts is the art of love.... Love is inspired by the Creator of nature. Love is a force of the soul that leads it as by a natural weight to its own place and end" (*De Natura et dignitate amoris* 1: PL 184, 379). Learning to love is a long and demanding process that is structured by William in four stages, corresponding to the ages of the human being: childhood, youth, maturity, and old-age. On this journey the person must impose upon himself an effective ascesis, firm self-control to eliminate every irregular affection, every capitulation to selfishness, and to unify his own life in God, the source, goal, and force of love, until he reaches the summit of the spiritual life which William calls "wisdom". At the end of this ascetic process, the person feels deep serenity and sweetness. All the human being's faculties—intelligence, will, affection—rest in God, known and loved in Christ.

In other works, too, William speaks of this radical vocation to love for God which is the secret of a successful and happy life and which he describes as a ceaseless, growing desire, inspired by God himself in the human heart. In a meditation, he says "that the object of this love is Love" with a capital "L", namely, God. It is he who pours himself out into the hearts of those who love him and prepares them to receive him. "God gives himself until the person is sated and in such a way that the desire is never lacking. This impetus of love is the fulfillment of the human being" (*De Contemplando Deo* 6, *passim*, *SC* 61 bis, pp. 79–83). The considerable importance that William gives to the emotional dimension is striking. Basically, dear friends, our hearts are made of flesh and blood, and when we love God, who is Love itself, how can we fail to express in this relationship with the Lord our most human feelings, such as tenderness, sensitivity, and delicacy? In becoming man, the Lord himself wanted to love us with a heart of flesh!

Moreover, according to William, love has another important quality: it illuminates the mind and enables one to know God better and more profoundly and, in God, people and events. The knowledge that proceeds from the senses and the intelligence reduces but does not eliminate the distance between the subject and the object, between the "I" and the "you". Love, on the other hand, gives rise to attraction and communion, to the point that transformation and assimilation take place between the subject who loves and the beloved object. This reciprocity of affection and liking subsequently permits a far deeper knowledge than that which is brought by reason alone. A famous saying of William expresses it: "*Amor ipse intellectus est*—love in itself is already the beginning of knowledge." Dear friends, let us ask ourselves: is not our life just like this? Is it not perhaps true that we only truly know *who* and *what* we love? Without a certain fondness, one knows no one and nothing! And this applies first of all to the knowledge of God and his mysteries, which exceed our mental capacity to understand: God is known if he is loved!

A synthesis of William of Saint-Thierry's thought is contained in a long letter addressed to the Carthusians of Mont-Dieu, whom he visited and wished to encourage and console. Already in 1690, the learned Benedictine Jean Mabillon gave this letter a meaningful title: *Epistola Aurea* (Golden epistle). In fact, the teachings on spiritual life that it contains are invaluable for all those who wish to increase in communion with God and in holiness. In this treatise, William proposes an itinerary in three stages. It is necessary, he says, to move on from the "animal" being to the "rational" one, in order to attain to the "spiritual". What does our author mean by these three terms? To start with, a person accepts the vision of life inspired by faith with an act of obedience and trust. Then, with a process of interiorization, in which the reason and the will play an important role, faith in Christ is received with profound conviction, and one feels a harmonious correspondence between what is believed and what is hoped and the most secret aspirations of the soul, our reason, our affections. One therefore arrives at the perfection of spiritual life when the realities of faith are a source of deep joy and real and satisfying communion with God. One lives only in love and for love. William based this process on a solid vision of the human being inspired by the ancient Greek Fathers, especially Origen, who, with bold language, taught that the human being's vocation was to become like God, who created him in his image and likeness. The image of God present in man impels him toward likeness, that is, toward an ever fuller identity between his own will and the divine will. One does not attain this perfection, which William calls "unity of spirit", by one's own efforts, even if they are sincere and generous, because something else is necessary. This perfection is reached through the action of the Holy Spirit, who takes up his abode in the soul and purifies, absorbs, and transforms into charity every impulse and desire of love that is present in the human being. "Then there is a further likeness to God", we read in the *Epistola Aurea*, "which is no longer called 'likeness' but 'unity of spirit', when the person becomes one with God, one in spirit, not only because of the unity of an identical desire, but through being unable to desire anything else. In this way the human being deserves to become not God but what God is: man becomes through grace what God is by nature" (*Epistola Aurea* 262–263, SC 223, pp. 353–355).

Dear brothers and sisters, this author, whom we might describe as the "Singer of Charity, of Love", teaches us to make the basic decision in our lives which gives meaning and value to all our other decisions: to love God and, through love of him, to love our neighbor; only in this manner shall we be able to find true joy, an anticipation of eternal beatitude. Let us therefore learn from the Saints in order to learn to love authentically and totally, to set our being on this journey. Together with a young Saint, a Doctor of the Church, Thérèse of the Child Jesus, let us tell the Lord that we, too, want to live on love. And I conclude with a prayer precisely by this Saint: "You know I love you, Jesus Christ, my Own! Your Spirit's fire of love enkindles me. By loving you, I draw the Father here, down to my heart, to stay with me always. Blessed Trinity! You are my prisoner dear,

of love, today. . . . To live on love, 'tis without stint to give.
And never count the cost, nor ask reward. . . . O Heart
Divine, o'erflowing with tenderness, How swift I run, who
all to You have given! Naught but your love I need, my life
to bless" [To live on love].

33

Rupert of Deutz

WEDNESDAY, 9 DECEMBER 2009
Paul VI Audience Hall

Dear Brothers and Sisters,

Today we become acquainted with another twelfth-century Benedictine monk. His name is Rupert of Deutz, a city near Cologne, home to a famous monastery. Rupert himself speaks of his own life in one of his most important works, entitled *The Glory and Honor of the Son of Man* [*De gloria et honore filii hominis super Matthaeum*], which is a commentary on part of the Gospel according to Matthew. While still a boy he was received at the Benedictine Monastery of Saint Laurence at Lièges as an "oblate", in accordance with the custom at that time of entrusting one of the sons to the monks for his education, intending to make him a gift to God. Rupert always loved monastic life. He quickly learned Latin in order to study the Bible and to enjoy the liturgical celebrations. He was distinguished by his unswerving moral rectitude and his strong attachment to the See of Saint Peter.

Rupert's time was marked by disputes between the Papacy and the Empire, because of the so-called "Investiture Controversy" with which—as I have mentioned in other Catecheses—the Papacy wished to prevent the appointment of Bishops and the exercise of their jurisdiction from depending on the civil authorities, who were certainly not guided by pastoral reasons but for the most part by political and financial considerations. Bishop Otbert of Lièges resisted the Pope's directives and exiled Berengarius, Abbot of the Monastery of Saint Laurence, because of his fidelity to the Pontiff. It was in this monastery that Rupert lived. He did not hesitate to follow his Abbot into exile, and only when Bishop Otbert returned to communion with the Pope did he return to Liège and agree to become a priest. Until that moment, in fact, he had avoided receiving ordination from a Bishop in dissent with the Pope. Rupert teaches us that when controversies arise in the Church, the reference to the Petrine ministry guarantees fidelity to sound doctrine and is a source of serenity and inner freedom. After the dispute with Otbert, Rupert was obliged to leave his monastery again twice. In 1116 his adversaries even wanted to take him to court. Although he was acquitted of every accusation, Rupert preferred to go for a while to Siegburg; but since on his return to the monastery in Liège the disputes had not yet ceased, he decided to settle definitively in Germany. In 1120 he was appointed Abbot of Deutz, where, except for making a pilgrimage to Rome in 1124, he lived until 1129, the year of his death.

A fertile writer, Rupert left numerous works, still today of great interest because he played an active part in various important theological discussions of his time. For example, he intervened with determination in the Eucharistic controversy, which in 1077 led to his condemnation by Berengarius of Tours. Berengarius had given a reductive interpretation of Christ's presence in the Sacrament of the Eucharist, describing it as merely symbolic. In the language of the Church, the term "transubstantiation" was as yet unknown, but Rupert, at times with daring words, made himself a staunch supporter of the Eucharistic reality and, especially in a work entitled *De divinis officiis* (On divine offices), purposefully asserted the continuity between the Body of the Incarnate Word of Christ and that present in the Eucharistic species of the bread and the wine. Dear brothers and sisters, it seems to me that at this point we must also think of our time; today, too, we are in danger of reappraising the Eucharistic reality, that is, of considering the Eucharist almost as a rite of communion, of socialization alone, forgetting all too easily that the Risen Christ is really present in the Eucharist with his Risen Body, which is placed in our hands *to draw us out* of ourselves, *to incorporate us* into his immortal body, and thereby to *lead us* to new life. This great mystery that the Lord is present in his full reality in the Eucharistic species is a mystery to be adored and loved ever anew! I would like here to quote the words of the *Catechism of the Catholic Church* which bear the fruit of two thousand years of meditation on the faith and theological reflection: "The mode of Christ's presence under the Eucharistic species is unique and incomparable. . . . In the most blessed sacrament of the Eucharist 'the Body and Blood, together with the soul and divinity, of our Lord Jesus Christ . . . is truly, really, and substantially contained'. . . . It is a substantial presence by which Christ, God and man, makes himself wholly and entirely present . . . by the conversion of the bread and wine into Christ's body and blood" (cf. nos. 1374–1375). Rupert, too, contributed with his reflections to this precise formulation.

Another controversy in which the Abbot of Deutz was involved concerns the problem of the reconciliation of God's goodness and omnipotence with the existence of evil. If God is omnipotent and good, how is it possible to explain the reality of evil? Rupert, in fact, reacted to the position

assumed by the teachers of the theological school of Laon,
who, with a series of philosophical arguments, distinguished in God's will the "to approve" and the "to permit", concluding that God permits evil without approving
it and hence without desiring it. Rupert, on the other hand,
renounces the use of philosophy, which he deems inade-
quate for addressing such a great problem, and remains simply faithful to the biblical narration. He starts with the
goodness of God, with the truth that God is supremely good
and cannot desire anything but good. Thus he identifies
the origin of evil in the human being himself and in the
erroneous use of human freedom. When Rupert addresses
this topic, he writes pages filled with religious inspiration
to praise the Father's infinite mercy, God's patience with
the sinful human being, and his kindness to him.

Like other medieval theologians, Rupert, too, wondered
why the Word of God, the Son of God, was made man.
Some, many, answered by explaining the Incarnation of the
Word by the urgent need to atone for human sin. Rupert,
on the other hand, with a Christocentric vision of salvation history, broadens the perspective and, in a work entitled *The Glorification of the Trinity*, sustains the position that
the Incarnation, the central event of the whole of history,
was planned from eternity, even independently of human
sin, so that the whole Creation might praise God the Father
and love him as one family gathered round Christ, the Son
of God. Then he saw in the pregnant woman of the Apocalypse the entire history of humanity, which is oriented to
Christ, just as conception is oriented to birth, a perspective
that was to be developed by other thinkers and enhanced
by contemporary theology, which says that the whole history of the world and of humanity is a conception oriented
to the birth of Christ. Christ is always the center of the

exegetic explanations provided by Rupert in his commentaries on the Books of the Bible, to which he dedicated himself with great diligence and passion. Thus, he rediscovers a wonderful unity in all the events of the history of salvation, from the Creation until the final consummation of time: "All Scripture", he says, "is one book, which aspires to the same end (the divine Word); which comes from one God and was written by one Spirit" (*De glorificatione Trinitatis et procesione Sancti spiritus* I, V: *PL* 169, 18).

In the interpretation of the Bible, Rupert did not limit himself to repeating the teaching of the Fathers, but shows an originality of his own. For example, he is the first writer to have identified the bride in the Song of Songs with Mary Most Holy. His commentary on this Book of Scripture has thus turned out to be a sort of Mariological *summa*, in which he presents Mary's privileges and excellent virtues. In one of the most inspired passages of his commentary, Rupert writes: "O most beloved among the beloved, Virgin of virgins, what does your beloved Son so praise in you that the whole choir of angels exalts? What they praise is your simplicity, purity, innocence, doctrine, modesty, humility, integrity of mind and body, that is, your incorrupt virginity" (*In Canticum Canticorum* 4, 1–6: *CCL* 26, pp. 69–70). The Marian interpretation of Rupert's *Canticum* is a felicitous example of harmony between liturgy and theology. In fact, various passages of this Book of the Bible were already used in liturgical celebrations on Marian feasts.

Rupert, furthermore, was careful to insert his Mariological doctrine into that ecclesiological doctrine. That is to say, he saw in Mary Most Holy the holiest part of the whole Church. For this reason, my venerable Predecessor, Pope Paul VI, in his Discourse for the closure of the third session of the Second Vatican Council, in solemnly pronouncing

Mary Mother of the Church, even cited a phrase taken from Rupert's works, which describes Mary as *portio maxima, portio optima*—the most sublime part, the very best part of the Church (cf. *In Apocalypsem* 1, 7: PL 169, 1043).

Dear friends, from these brief allusions we realize that Rupert was a fervent theologian endowed with great depth. Like all the representatives of monastic theology, he was able to combine rational study of the mysteries of faith with prayer and contemplation, which he considered the summit of all knowledge of God. He himself sometimes speaks of his mystical experiences, such as when he confides his ineffable joy at having perceived the Lord's presence: "in that brief moment", he says, "I experienced how true what he himself says is. *Learn from me for I am meek and humble of heart*" (*De gloria et honore Filii hominis. Super Matthaeum* 12: PL 1168, 1601). We, too, each one of us in his own way, can encounter the Lord Jesus who ceaselessly accompanies us on our way, makes himself present in the Eucharistic Bread and in his Word for our salvation.

34

John of Salisbury

WEDNESDAY, 16 DECEMBER 2009
Paul VI Audience Hall

Dear Brothers and Sisters,

Today we shall become acquainted with John of Salisbury, who belonged to one of the most important schools of philosophy and theology of the Middle Ages, that of the Cathedral of Chartres in France. Like the theologians of whom I have spoken in the past few weeks, John, too, helps us understand that faith, in harmony with the just aspirations of reason, impels thought toward the revealed truth in which is found the true good of the human being.

John was born in Salisbury, England, between 1100 and 1120. In reading his works, and especially the large collection of his letters, we learn about the most important events in his life. For about twelve years, from 1136 to 1148, he devoted himself to study, attending the best schools of his day, where he heard the lectures of famous teachers. He went to Paris and then to Chartres, the environment that made the greatest impression on his formation and from which he assimilated his great cultural openness, his interest in speculative problems, and his appreciation of literature. As often happened in that time, the most brilliant students were chosen by prelates and sovereigns to be their

close collaborators. This also happened to John of Salisbury, who was introduced to Theobald, Archbishop of
Canterbury—the Primatial See of England—by a great friend
of his, Bernard of Clairvaux. Theobald was glad to welcome John among his clergy. For eleven years, from 1150
to 1161, John was the secretary and chaplain of the elderly
Archbishop. With unflagging zeal he continued to devote
himself to study; he carried out an intense diplomatic activity, going to Italy ten times for the explicit purpose of fostering relations between the Kingdom and Church of
England and the Roman Pontiff. Moreover, the Pope in
those years was Adrian IV, an Englishman who was a close
friend of John of Salisbury. In the years following Adrian
IV's death, in 1159, a situation of serious tension arose in
England between the Church and the Kingdom. In fact,
King Henry II wished to impose his authority on the inter-
nal life of the Church, curtailing her freedom. This stance
provoked John of Salisbury to react and, in particular,
prompted the valiant resistance of Saint Thomas Becket,
Theobald's successor on the episcopal throne of Canterbury, who for this reason was exiled to France. John of
Salisbury accompanied him and remained in his service,
working ceaselessly for reconciliation. In 1170, when both
John and Thomas Becket had returned to England, Thomas
was attacked and murdered in his cathedral. He died a martyr and was immediately venerated as such by the people.
John continued to serve faithfully the successor of Thomas
as well, until he was appointed Bishop of Chartres, where
he lived from 1176 until 1180, the year of his death.

I would like to point out two of John of Salisbury's works
that are considered his masterpieces, bearing elegant Greek
titles: *Metalogicon* (In defense of logic) and *Policraticus* (The
man of government). In the first of these works, not without

that fine irony that is a feature of many scholars, he rejects the position of those who had a reductionist conception of culture, which they saw as empty eloquence and vain words. John, on the contrary, praises culture, authentic philosophy, that is, the encounter between rigorous thought and communication, effective words. He writes: "Indeed, just as eloquence that is not illuminated by reason is not only rash but blind, so wisdom that does not profit from the use of words is not only weak but in a certain way mutilated. Indeed, although, at times, wisdom without words might serve to square the individual with his own conscience, it is of rare or little profit to society" (*Metalogicon* I, I: *PL* 199, 327). This is a very timely teaching. Today, what John described as "eloquence", that is, the possibility of communicating with increasingly elaborate and widespread means, has increased enormously. Yet the need to communicate messages endowed with "wisdom", that is, inspired by truth, goodness, and beauty, is more urgent than ever. This is a great responsibility that calls into question in particular the people who work in the multiform and complex world of culture, of communications, of the *media*. And this is a realm in which the Gospel can be proclaimed with missionary zeal.

In the *Metalogicon*, John treats the problems of logic, in his day a subject of great interest, and asks himself a fundamental question: what can human reason know? To what point can it correspond with the aspiration that exists in every person, namely, to seek the truth? John of Salisbury adopts a moderate position, based on the teaching of certain treatises of Aristotle and Cicero. In his opinion, human reason normally attains knowledge that is not indisputable but probable and arguable. Human knowledge—this is his conclusion—is imperfect, because it is subject to finiteness, to human limitations. Nevertheless it grows and is perfected, thanks to the experience and elaboration of correct and consistent reasoning, able to make connections between concepts and the reality, through discussion, exchanges, and knowledge that is enriched from one generation to the next. Only in God is there perfect knowledge, which is communicated to the human being, at least partially, by means of Revelation received in faith, which is why the knowledge of faith, theology, unfolds the potential of reason and makes it possible to advance with humility in the knowledge of God's mysteries.

The believer and the theologian who deepen the treasure of faith also open themselves to a practical knowledge that guides our daily activity, in other words, moral law and the exercise of the virtues. John of Salisbury writes: "God's clemency has granted us his law, which establishes what it is useful for us to know and points out to us what it is legitimate for us to know of God and what it is right to investigate. . . . In this law, in fact, the will of God is explained and revealed so that each one of us may know what he needs to do" (*Metalogicon* 4, 41: *PL* 199, 944–945). According to John of Salisbury, an immutable objective truth also exists, whose origin is in God, accessible to human reason, and which concerns practical and social action. It is a natural law that must inspire human laws and political and religious authorities, so that they may promote the common good. This natural law is characterized by a property that John calls "equity", that is, the attribution to each person of his own rights. From this stem precepts that are legitimate for all peoples, and in no way can they be abrogated. This is the central thesis of *Policraticus*, the treatise of philosophy and political theology in which John of Salisbury reflects on the conditions that render government leaders just and acceptable.

Whereas other arguments addressed in this work are linked to the historical circumstances in which it was composed, the theme of the relationship between natural law and a positive juridical order, mediated by equity, is still of great importance today. In our time, in fact, especially in some countries, we are witnessing a disturbing divergence between reason, whose task is to discover the ethical values linked to the dignity of the human person, and freedom, whose responsibility is to accept and promote them. Perhaps John of Salisbury would remind us today that the only laws in conformity with equity are those that protect the sacredness of human life and reject the licitness of abortion, euthanasia, and bold genetic experimentation, those laws that respect the dignity of marriage between a man and a woman, that are inspired by a correct secularism of the State—a secularism that always entails the safeguard of religious freedom—and that pursue subsidiarity and solidarity at both the national and the international level. If this were not so, what John of Salisbury terms the "tyranny of princes", or as we would say, "the dictatorship of relativism", would end by coming to power, a relativism, as I recalled a few years ago, "which does not recognize anything as definitive and whose ultimate goal consists solely of one's own ego and desires" (Cardinal Joseph Ratzinger, Dean of the College of Cardinals, *Homily, Mass for the Election of the Roman Pontiff*, 18 April 2005).

In my most recent Encyclical, *Caritas in Veritate*, in addressing people of good will who strive to ensure that social and political action are never separated from the objective truth about man and his dignity, I wrote: "Truth, and the love which it reveals, cannot be produced: they can only be received as a gift. Their ultimate source is not, and cannot be, mankind, but only God, who is himself Truth and Love.

This principle is extremely important for society and for development, since neither can be a purely human product; the vocation to development on the part of individuals and peoples is not based simply on human choice but is an intrinsic part of a plan that is prior to us and constitutes for all of us a duty to be freely accepted" (no. 52). We must seek and welcome this plan that precedes us, this truth of being, so that justice may be born, but we may find it and welcome it only with a heart, a will, and a reason purified in the light of God.

35

Peter Lombard

WEDNESDAY, 30 DECEMBER 2009
Paul VI Audience Hall

Dear Brothers and Sisters,

At this last Audience of the year, I would like to speak to you about Peter Lombard: he was a theologian who lived in the twelfth century and enjoyed great fame because one of his works, entitled the *Sentences*, was used as a theological manual for many centuries.

So who was Peter Lombard? Although the information on his life is scarce, it is possible to reconstruct the essential lines of his biography. He was born between the eleventh and twelfth centuries near Novara, in Northern Italy, in a region that once belonged to the Lombards. For this very reason he was surnamed "the Lombard". He belonged to a modest family, as we may deduce from the letter of introduction that Bernard of Clairvaux wrote to Gilduin, Superior of the Abbey of Saint-Victor in Paris, asking him to give free accommodation to Peter, who wanted to go to that city in order to study. In fact, even in the Middle Ages, not only nobles or the rich might study and acquire important roles in ecclesial and social life, but also people of humble origin, such as, for example, Gregory VII, the Pope who stood up to Emperor Henry VI, or Maurice of Sully, the Archbishop of Paris who commissioned the building of Notre-Dame and who was the son of a poor peasant.

Peter Lombard began his studies in Bologna and then went to Rheims and lastly to Paris. From 1140, he taught at the prestigious school of Notre-Dame. Esteemed and appreciated as a theologian, eight years later he was charged by Pope Eugene II to examine the doctrine of Gilbert de la Porrée that was giving rise to numerous discussions because it was held to be not wholly orthodox. Having become a priest, he was appointed Bishop of Paris in 1159, a year before his death in 1160.

Like all theology teachers of his time, Peter also wrote discourses and commentaries on Sacred Scripture. His masterpiece, however, consists of the four books of the *Sentences*. This is a text which came into being for didactic purposes. According to the theological method in use in those times, it was necessary first of all to know, study, and comment on the thought of the Fathers of the Church and of the other writers deemed authoritative. Peter, therefore, collected a very considerable amount of documentation, which consisted mainly of the teachings of the great Latin Fathers, especially Saint Augustine, and was open to the contribution of contemporary theologians. Among other things, he also used an encyclopedia of Greek theology which had only recently become known to the West: *The Orthodox Faith*, composed by Saint John Damascene. The great merit of Peter Lombard is to have organized all the material that he had collected and chosen with care in a systematic and harmonious framework. In fact, one of the features of theology is to organize the patrimony of faith in a unitive and orderly way. Thus he distributed the *sentences*, that is, the Patristic sources on various arguments, in four books. In the first book he addresses God and the Trinitarian mystery; in the second, the work of the Creation, sin, and grace; in the third, the mystery of the Incarnation and the work of redemption with an extensive exposition on the virtues. The fourth book is dedicated to the sacraments and to the last realities, those of eternal life, or *Novissimi*. The overall view presented includes almost all the truths of the Catholic faith. The concise, clear vision and clear, orderly, schematic, and ever consistent presentation explain the extraordinary success of Peter Lombard's *Sentences*. They enabled students to learn reliably and gave the educators and teachers who used them plenty of room for acquiring deeper knowledge. A Franciscan theologian, Alexandre of Hales, of the next generation, introduced into the *Sentences* a division that facilitated their study and consultation. Even the greatest of the thirteenth-century theologians, Albert the Great, Bonaventure of Bagnoregio, and Thomas Aquinas, began their academic activity by commenting on the four books of Peter Lombard's *Sentences*, enriching them with their reflections. Lombard's text was the book in use at all schools of theology until the sixteenth century.

I would like to emphasize how the organic presentation of faith is an indispensable requirement. In fact, the individual truths of faith illuminate each other and, in their total and unitive vision, the harmony of God's plan of salvation and the centrality of the mystery of Christ become evident. After the example of Peter Lombard, I invite all theologians and priests always to keep in mind the whole vision of the Christian doctrine, to counter today's risks of fragmentation and the depreciation of the individual truths. The *Catechism of the Catholic Church*, as well as the *Compendium* of this same Catechism, offer us precisely this full picture of Christian Revelation, to be accepted with faith and gratitude. I would therefore like to encourage the individual faithful and the

Christian communities to make the most of these instruments to know and to deepen the content of our faith. It will thus appear to us as a marvelous symphony that speaks to us of God and of his love and asks of us firm adherence and an active response.

To get an idea of the interest that the reading of Peter Lombard's *Sentences* still inspires today, I propose two examples. Inspired by Saint Augustine's Commentary on the Book of Genesis, Peter wonders why woman was created from man's rib and not from his head or his feet. And Peter explains: "She was formed neither as a dominator nor as a slave of man but rather as his companion" (*Sentences* 3, 18, 3). Then, still on the basis of the Patristic teaching, he adds: "The mystery of Christ and of the Church is represented in this act. Just as, in fact, woman was formed from Adam's rib while he slept, so the Church was born from the sacraments that began to flow from the side of Christ, asleep on the Cross, that is, from the blood and water with which we are redeemed from sin and cleansed of guilt" (*Sentences* 3, 18, 4). These are profound reflections that still apply today, when the theology and spirituality of Christian marriage have considerably deepened the analogy with the spousal relationship of Christ and his Church.

In another passage in one of his principal works, Peter Lombard, treating the merits of Christ, asks himself: "Why, then, does [Christ] wish to suffer and die, if his virtues were sufficient to obtain for himself all the merits?" His answer is incisive and effective: "For you, not for himself!" He then continues with another question and another answer, which seem to reproduce the discussions that went on during the lessons of medieval theology teachers: "And in what sense did he suffer and die for me? So that his Passion and his death might be an example and cause for you. An example of virtue and humility, a cause of glory and freedom; an example given by God, obedient unto death; a cause of your liberation and your beatitude" (*Sentences* 3, 18, 5).

Among the most important contributions offered by Peter Lombard to the history of theology, I would like to recall his treatise on the sacraments, of which he gave what I would call a definitive definition: "One calls a sacrament in the proper sense precisely that which is a sign of God's grace and a visible form of invisible grace, in such a way that it bears its image and is its cause" (4, 1, 4). With this definition, Peter Lombard grasps the essence of the sacraments: they are a cause of grace; they are truly able to communicate divine life. Subsequent theologians never again departed from this vision and were also to use the distinction between the material and the formal element introduced by the "Master of the Sentences", as Peter Lombard was known. The material element is the tangible visible reality; the formal element consists of the words spoken by the minister. For a complete and valid celebration of the sacraments, both are essential: matter, the reality with which the Lord visibly touches us, and the word that conveys the spiritual significance. In Baptism, for example, the material element is the water that is poured on the head of the child, and the formal element is the formula: "I baptize you in the name of the Father, of the Son, and of the Holy Spirit." Peter the Lombard, moreover, explained that the sacraments alone objectively transmit divine grace, and they are seven: Baptism, the Eucharist, Penance, the Unction of the sick, Orders, and Matrimony (cf. *Sentences* 4, 2, 1).

Dear brothers and sisters, it is important to recognize how precious and indispensable for every Christian is the sacramental life in which the Lord transmits this matter in the community of the Church and touches and transforms us.

As the *Catechism of the Catholic Church* says, the sacraments are "powers that come forth from the Body of Christ, which is ever-living and life-giving. They are actions of the Holy Spirit" (no. 1116). In this Year for Priests which we are celebrating, I urge priests, especially ministers in charge of souls, to have an intense sacramental life themselves in the first place in order to be of help to the faithful. May the celebration of the sacraments be characterized by dignity and decorum, encourage personal recollection and community participation, the sense of God's presence and missionary zeal. The sacraments are the great treasure of the Church, and it is the task of each one of us to celebrate them with spiritual profit. In them an ever-amazing event touches our lives: Christ, through the visible signs, comes to us, purifies us, transforms us, and makes us share in his divine friendship

Dear friends, we have come to the end of this year and to the threshold of the New Year. I hope that the friendship of Our Lord Jesus Christ will accompany you every day of this year that is about to begin. May Christ's friendship be our light and guide, helping us to be people of peace, of his peace. Happy New Year to you all!